EXCEL STILL MORE

DAILY BIBLE DEVOTIONAL

VOLUME 1 · THE FOUR GOSPELS

KRIS EMERSON

Published by
Spiritbuilding Publishers
9700 Ferry Road, Waynesville, OH 45068
(800) 282-4901

ESM DAILY BIBLE DEVOTIONAL:
Volume 1 – The Four Gospels:
by Kris Emerson

Printed in the United States of America

ISBN: 978-1964805085

Spiritbuilding

PUBLISHERS

spiritbuilding.com

INTRODUCTION

Daily Bible reading is crucial to growing in the grace and knowledge of our Lord Jesus Christ. The goal of reading extends beyond simply seeing the text on the page. Growth results from understanding the text, discerning the Holy Spirit's intent, and making practical applications that intensify daily living in Christ. The Excel Still More Daily Devotional is designed to help in all those areas.

Imagine starting every weekday morning in the New Testament. You read a chapter and quietly consider what God is showing you. The daily devotional book becomes a companion piece to facilitate more consideration of the text and a deeper appreciation for the revelation of God.

The first paragraph recaps the content of the daily reading. This section serves as a reminder of what is in the passage and links together the events and teachings from the text. When necessary, this section can supplement the daily read.

The second paragraph seeks to derive the application of the text. What is God expecting you to draw from what He has revealed? This section moves through the author's intent and into the practical application that can immediately affect your life.

The third paragraph is a prayer using the "we" pronouns. You and I will bow together, drawing from the theme and teachings of the chapter to communicate our thankfulness, needs, and desires to God. Let us go to our Father together.

The final section is a series of thought questions derived from the daily reading. These questions represent mediation and action questions to ensure the scripture is tangible in your daily decisions.

Excel Still More Podcast and Devotionals
sponsored by:

CONTENTS

If you would like any assistance in your study, or have prayer requests, please feel free to contact Kris Emerson directly at **emersonk78@me.com**.

MATTHEW 1

The book of Matthew opens with the lineage of Jesus through his earthly father Joseph. Tying Jesus back to King David, the tribe of Judah, and Abraham, is a powerful opening point for the Jewish reader. This means that Jesus is the One spoken of in the great promises God made to these mighty men of faith. Jesus is the Messiah for which they were waiting! If you are looking to get more out of this genealogy, take a pencil and box in the names you recognize. There are some great men and women of faith listed here. Following this, Matthew continues to confirm Jesus as the Savior from the prophets, by citing Isaiah and telling the story of Jesus being born of a virgin, just as the Hebrew Scripture taught.

FOR MY BENEFIT

God planned to send Christ to become "God with us" from the foundation of the world. He chose to carry this out through the nation of Israel. God was incredibly patient for 2000 years, dating back to the days of Abraham. Repeatedly, He promised that all would be blessed, a Ruler would be established, and His Son would be the Savior of His people. We are enjoying the fulfillment and substance of that promise. From the moment a virgin gave birth to a child, the world was changed. We are blessed as a result of that change. Praise be to God for waiting patiently, enduring lovingly, and sending His Son to save us.

MY PRAYER

Great Father of Abraham, Judah, and David, we direct all praise and honor to Your mighty name. Thank you for working through the patriarchs, families, and kings to bring about "the Messiah" with His spiritual and eternal blessings. Thank you for Mary and Joseph's faith and for the wonderful moment when Your divine Son entered this world on our behalf. Please give us the humility to be grateful and the faith to live out the intent of Christ's coming. Show us what it means to be set apart as holy people: redeemed, purchased, and ruled by Your beloved Son.

THOUGHT QUESTIONS

How can you draw faith-building value from a study of genealogies? What does it mean that Matthew links well-known biblical figures together?

Why is the virgin prophecy of Isaiah 7:14 the right place to start building a case for Christ? How is the uniqueness of this miracle still potent today?

What will be different about your day because you know God patiently and meticulously planned out the coming of Christ for your benefit?

MATTHEW 2

Matthew documents the events immediately following Jesus' birth. From the worshiping magi to the conniving Herod to the angel sending the family to Egypt, everything culminates in the murderous rampage of the king killing all the young boys in Bethlehem. Following Herod's death, an angel directs Jesus' family back to Nazareth. The significance of this chapter is found in the prophecies. Micah states a Ruler will come from Bethlehem. Hosea tells of God's Son coming from Egypt. Jeremiah teaches there will be weeping at the loss of children. An unnamed prophet predicts that the Messiah will be called a Nazarene. Matthew is aligning the story of Jesus with the prophets of old. This would carry tremendous weight for the Jew and should demonstrate God's design and control to us as well.

FOR MY BENEFIT

God controls how things come together for the good of His will and His people. Before Jesus was born, God knew all things. He used prophets to confirm His power to us. Life was not easy for those whom God chose to be a part of this incredible story. Circumstances were hard for Joseph and Mary, and certainly for families who lost their children to Herod's wrath. But God was working on something beautiful and eternal. You are eternally blessed as the result of so much suffering and loss. God allowed this to save and bless you. Be thankful for those who labored in faith to bring about our Lord's victory and stand prepared to struggle in His honor.

MY PRAYER

Compassionate Father, thank You for the word of the prophets, confirming our faith in Jesus Christ. Thank You for the examples of sacrifice throughout the life of Jesus that have graciously invited us into the redemptive story with Him. Will you give us the wisdom to see how much you endured to establish spiritual life and hope? Help us to be grateful for Your willingness to keep working on us, even amid the efforts of evil men. And may we return thanks by being worshipful and obedient like the magi in the days of Jesus' birth.

THOUGHT QUESTIONS

How does it strengthen your faith to see the story of Christ being revealed through Old Testament prophecies? What do they prove?

What do you learn about faithfulness from the hardships of Joseph and Mary? What should you expect in your life of devotion to God?

How can you see God's power and goodness when babies were allowed to die at Herod's hand? How does it cast your eyes more toward eternity?

MATTHEW 3

The last chapter of the Old Testament, Malachi 4, concludes by announcing that God will send "Elijah the prophet before the coming of the great and terrible day of the LORD." Matthew reveals this man to be John the Baptist. He is Jesus' cousin, and he lays the foundation for the teachings of Jesus. His message includes vital kingdom elements: repentance of sins, baptism in water, the Holy Spirit, and the fire of judgment. Some who come to him want the ceremonial washing but are unwilling to repent or accept the whole gospel message. John is laying the crucial groundwork for that complete gospel. Jesus, the greater One, would come after him. This begins with John baptizing Jesus as the Spirit descends upon Him and the Father speaks in approval of His "beloved Son."

FOR MY BENEFIT

Our God wants everyone to be saved in Christ. Therefore, He is clear and concise when it comes to how to be saved. John the Baptist's teachings help us see that. Forgiveness of sins was available to anyone who turned from sin with repentant hearts, was baptized in water, and devoted their life to obeying the will of God and His Spirit, with a healthy fear of eternal fire. All of that can be stated in a simple and life-changing way: follow Jesus. He came to do what was right and honor His Father. He was baptized in water "to fulfill all righteousness." He then lived in the Spirit, full of grace and on a mission for God. In Him, so can we!

MY PRAYER

" Wonderful Father, You are above us and greater than us in every possible way. And yet, You have communicated Your will to us so simply and powerfully. Thank You for sending John the Baptist to pave the way for our Savior. Thank you for sending Jesus to be our example, our Teacher, and our victorious King. Help us to be open to the whole gospel in a way that surpasses the Pharisees. Encourage us to live out the teachings of Jesus and to follow His example in all that we do.

"

THOUGHT QUESTIONS

Does the word "repent" carry the same importance in your life as it did to Jesus and John? How do you demonstrate that?

_____

_____

Is baptism as important to you as it was to Jesus and John? Beyond initial obedience, how do you demonstrate baptism's importance?

_____

_____

Are you living by faith in the Godhead? How do you show love and honor for the Father, the Son, and the Holy Spirit in your daily life?

_____

_____

MATTHEW 4

It is difficult to imagine forty days without food. It is God's plan for the Holy Spirit to lead Jesus into the wilderness to fast for that length of time. The devil takes the opportunity to try and stop Jesus' redemptive ministry by tempting Him using three basic tactics: the lust of the eye, the lust of the flesh, and the pride of life. Each time Jesus refuses to listen and uses Scripture to refute him. Following this, an angel comes and comforts Jesus. Jesus then travels to Galilee to begin His ministry. He begins with this powerful sentence: "Repent for the kingdom of heaven is at hand." Jesus gathers up His first four apostles: Peter, Andrew, James, and John. He then goes about healing people and preaching "the gospel of the kingdom."

FOR MY BENEFIT

Satan is not particularly creative. When he tempted Jesus with stones to bread, with the world's glory, and with leaping from the temple, it was no different than the temptations Adam and Eve faced in the garden. He appeals to fleshly desires, distracted eyes, and a sense of importance. Adam failed. Jesus succeeded. In the footsteps of Jesus, with Scripture in our hearts and hands, we also can face temptation and stand with God. The result will be like Jesus: God will strengthen us, upholding our efforts, drawing us to people of faith who will walk with us, and opening opportunities to use our proven faith to share the gospel of the kingdom more boldly with others.

MY PRAYER

Great God of glory, thank you for sending Your Son to show us what it means to fully trust in You. Help us face our times in the wilderness with the same resolve to honor You in all circumstances. Will You give us the clarity we need to see through the devil's tactics? We pray for comfort and support from those who have faced Satan and stood firm. We also pray to be those traveling companions for others, as we share in our common mission of telling others what is possible through our Lord Jesus Christ.

THOUGHT QUESTIONS

Will you be aware today of Satan's three tools: the lust of the eyes, the lust of the flesh, and the boastful pride of life? How will awareness help?

_____

_____

How is facing temptation strengthened by quoting God's word? How will you use Scripture to refute the devil's work today?

_____

_____

Why is it vital to get to work for Christ immediately following temptation? What mission will you stay focused on today no matter what?

_____

_____

MATTHEW 5

Early in Jesus' ministry, He sits on a mountainside and gathers His disciples. In perhaps the most powerful sermon of all time, He explains to them the qualities of kingdom citizens. His kingdom would include people who lived differently from the world. Those differences would be seeded in the heart. To show this, Jesus begins with what we call "the Beatitudes." Qualities like humility, gentleness, and internal hunger for righteousness would define His people. Such hearts would explode into lives of great light for Christ, become salt upon the earth, and show righteousness that far surpasses the Jewish leaders of their day. Faithfulness would be as much about what you feel toward others as how you end up treating them, even enemies! Jesus is teaching that faithfulness begins with love.

FOR MY BENEFIT

The sermon on the mount is incredibly valuable for believers. We must think and feel differently than this world, especially in the face of trials. We live so that Christ's light shines through us, beginning deep within our hearts. We do not murder, but we also do not gossip. We do not commit adultery, but we also do not lust in our hearts. We do not retaliate, but we also seek to serve others. In many ways, the disciples of Jesus were counterculture, and continue to be today. Our first step of faith in God is to deny self. God loves all men and seeks to save them, and we should feel the same and be workers in His Son's kingdom.

MY PRAYER

Heavenly Father, thank You for sending Your Son to come to this earth and show us Your character and heart. As Jesus taught us of His nature, we pray to take on His heart as our own. Lord, help us to be humble, to be gentle, to be pure in heart, and peacemakers. Give us opportunities to shine, even if that requires us to walk by faith in places of darkness. Give us the desire to do good to others out of love for You and for them, even our enemies. Please perfect us in Your love.

THOUGHT QUESTIONS

How important are the beatitudes in setting the stage for you to shine and make a difference? Which one will you focus on today?

_____

_____

Are you ready to accept that you are the reflection of Christ's light in this world? How will your choices today bring glory to Him?

_____

_____

How are disciples to be more righteous than Pharisees? Will you determine today to check your heart and do things for the right reasons?

_____

_____

MATTHEW 6

As the sermon on the mount continues, Jesus explains that righteousness is not just about what we do, but also why we do it. To illustrate, Jesus uses three examples: giving, praying, and fasting. Charity is a staple in the disciple's life, but it must be for God and others, not ourselves. Prayer is a powerful testimony of faith, but it must be about fellowship with God, not the praise of others. Fasting is about focusing on God, not impressing others. This is all about treasure in heaven with God, not this earth. Jesus' disciples are not worried about the things of this life because they live for heaven. They trust in God, live for Him, and know that He will take care of them if they seek Him above all else.

FOR MY BENEFIT

Jesus touches on sensitive topics in this chapter: giving to the poor, praying faithfully, and fasting from things to give attention to God. These are all challenges in our busy lives. How can we grow in them? Start from a place of love for God and others, and then be thankful for these outlets of praise. Carry that heart into the area of money and worry as well. These have choked out the word in many lives. We cannot serve God and money. We cannot live in anxiety and be courageous in Christ. Put His kingdom first, pray continually, and allow the Spirit to mold you, practicing righteousness from the heart, one day at a time. Do not worry about tomorrow.

MY PRAYER

Righteous God, teach us to yearn to serve You daily. Help us to give to others as You bountifully give to us. Humble us to pray privately, grateful that You listen. Strengthen us to fast from earthly things, so we can show You are first in our lives. May we live to store up eternal treasures. Thank you for Christ's spiritual victory, so we know that life is more than money and possessions and that there is no reason to worry over earthly things. We will seek You first and cast aside worry and fear in Jesus' name.

THOUGHT QUESTIONS

Why do you do righteous things? From charity work to prayer to fasting, how should that be centrally about God and your love for Him?

How does "the Lord's Prayer" place you in the right state of mind to take on the day in faith? What piece of it means the most to you today?

Are God's people different when it comes to the allure of wealth and the worries of an uncertain world? How? What sustains us in all of that?

MATTHEW 7

Jesus concludes His timeless sermon by challenging disciples to think properly about judgment. Judging others sometimes drifts into God's side of things. And many times people are judging from a place of deception about themselves. In other words, they do not see things clearly, and their judgment is clouded. Jesus tells His disciples to examine themselves and pray fervently for God to help them, to give them clarity, and to make them who they need to be. Perhaps from that place, one can weigh the deeds of another. Few are willing to be so humble. And few will be saved. Many will be like the false prophets in their motives. But not Jesus' disciples. They will hear Christ and seek to obey Him and be like Him in all they do.

FOR MY BENEFIT

Passing judgment on others is a temptation we all face. Sometimes it is done in sincerity and with their best interest at heart. But all too often it may say more about our shortcomings as the one judging. Always be humble. Always start by looking to yourself and follow that closely with a prayer to God. Ask God for clarity, wisdom, and help to love others by doing what is right toward them. Determine what to do to others by what you would have them do to you. In the end, look for proper fruit in yourself and them. Hear Jesus and do God's will, and you will be on a solid foundation in every situation, in both calm and storm.

MY PRAYER

Holy heavenly Father, all praise to You for your kindness and patience in how you judge Your servants. Thank You for always being near us, for hearing our prayers, and for giving us good gifts. Dear Lord, empower us to bear good fruit in Your honor. We know this means doing Your will and being more like Jesus. We ask for help in doing that, especially when it comes to treating others with patience and mercy. In every season, in sunshine or storm, we will put our trust in You and stand upon the foundation of Your Son.

THOUGHT QUESTIONS

What does "do not judge" mean to you? Are you careful to treat people the same way you would have them treat you?

_____

_____

Are you turning to God in prayer to ask for wisdom before addressing others? Can we bear good fruit without God's daily and personal help?

_____

_____

Will you act on the will of Jesus today? What is one thing from the sermon on the mount that you can stand upon to face life's daily storms?

_____

_____

MATTHEW 8

Matthew's gospel has a purposeful structure to build out the authority of Jesus. Chapters 1-4 tell the story of Jesus in prophecy. Chapters 5-7 are filled with Jesus' life-changing teachings. Now, in chapters 8-9, the focus is placed squarely on miracles. In today's short chapter, we are gifted the following stories: the healing of the leper, the healing of the Centurion's servant, the healing of Peter's mother-in-law, the calming of the sea of Galilee, and the demons cast into the swine. This list forms a dynamic way of showing the power of Jesus over all things. Upon closer examination, it shows He can heal the body, He has authority over space and time, He overpowers the spiritual forces of darkness, and even the natural world obeys His mighty will.

FOR MY BENEFIT

Where can we go to escape the jurisdiction of Jesus? And why would we even try? These stories give us tremendous confidence in how Christ can benefit our lives. As a man was burdened with decay through leprosy, so are we with physical sickness and spiritual death. Jesus, filled with compassion, promises to heal us of spiritual disease, and often helps with our physical needs! Jesus casting out demons reminds us that He is mightier than Satan and his workers. Without Christ's power and presence, we would be helpless in the spiritual warfare beyond our sight as well as the daily storms of life. Jesus alone has the might to protect us. May we put our faith and trust in Him.

MY PRAYER

“ *Oh Great God of majesty, may we take a moment today and be in awe of Your limitless power over all things. Thank you for demonstrating Your might through Jesus Christ. The natural world, the spiritual world, the human body, and the soul, are all subject to the glory and ability of Jesus. May our faith never limit the display of His power. Father, the storms of life often distract us. Help us to never give in to fear, but to turn to our Savior and call upon His presence to calm the storm and hold us close.* ”

THOUGHT QUESTIONS

What will happen if you approach Jesus with your sins like the leper in today's chapter? How does Jesus respond to such humility?

How far does the authority of Jesus reach? Is there any request you can make in faith that will be too much for Jesus? Go for it!

If Jesus controls the storms and the demons, two things outside of you and beyond your control, how should that affect how you pray today?

MATTHEW 9

This chapter furthers Matthew's mission of demonstrating the glory of Christ through miracles. Like the previous chapter, he lists quite a few of them: Jesus heals the paralytic, He heals the woman with 12 years of blood flow, He raises a young lady from the dead, heals two blind men, and casts out demons! The purpose of these miracles is to demonstrate some wonderful things about Jesus. First, He is compassionate. He feels for people and seeks to help them. Second, He has the power to cleanse souls of sin! The physical miracles prove His miraculous power to do all things. Third, this chapter continues to prove that there are no limits to Jesus' authority. He controls the body and soul, life and death, and the physical and spiritual realm.

FOR MY BENEFIT

Jesus is the most wonderful gift the world has ever known. But some religious leaders refused to accept Him. They question His ability to forgive sins. They question why He dined with sinners. They even attribute His healing power to demons! They were jealous and selfish and refused to trust in Jesus and give Him the control He deserved. May you and I never let our limited knowledge and understanding foster such doubt. Contrary to these men, a desperate woman was healed, and another was raised from death by simple, trusting faith in Jesus as God's Son. Christ acts in our lives because of our faith. May we be less like the Pharisees and more like those humble, blessed believers!

MY PRAYER

" Heavenly Father, God of compassion, thank You for sending Your Son to show the world the perfect combination of power and mercy. Thank You for His willingness to feel compassion for those hurting spiritually, physically, and emotionally. Help us to see how beautifully Christ demonstrates His authority to heal and help and comfort those who fully put their trust in Him. May we be those people today, in prayer and faithfulness to Him. Lord, the harvest is plentiful. There are so many struggling and in need of Jesus. Give us the humility, selflessness, and boldness to share His name openly with others. "

THOUGHT QUESTIONS

Has Jesus proven to you that He has the power and willingness to forgive your sins? If so, how will you approach Him in prayer today?

_____

_____

How can we sometimes be like the Pharisees in how we see others, misunderstanding how desperately Jesus wants everyone to be saved?

_____

_____

Do you have compassion for the hurting? If this Christ-like quality is in you, what can you do today to spread the love of Jesus to another?

_____

_____

MATTHEW 10

Jesus summons the twelve apostles and gives them the power to work miracles. He sends them out to the Jewish people to preach the coming kingdom of Christ. This becomes an early lesson to the disciples that some will openly embrace the gospel, but many will not. He notes that they are like sheep sent out amidst the wolves. But even under persecution, they are told "Do not worry" for the Holy Spirit of God is with them. If Jesus was rejected by some, so too will they be rejected. Do not fear what man can do to you. Only fear God who sees and knows all. The Gospel will unite some in joy, but it will also be a sword of division for others, even in one's own household.

FOR MY BENEFIT

The most uttered instruction in Scripture is this: "Do not be afraid." Twice it is spoken of in today's read. The call to discipleship is not one of ease. If it was, Christians would not be tempted to fear. The disciples were given the most wonderful tools: the approval of Jesus, power from heaven, and the Holy Spirit. They were then challenged to use those tools to herald the coming kingdom in this world. That mission would draw negativity and persecution. And so it will be for you and me. Being on a mission means sharing the Light of Christ in this dark world. This can lead to trouble. Even so, we must boldly take up our cross and follow Jesus.

MY PRAYER

All-knowing God and Father, give us the faith and wisdom today to know You are with us. Help us to live courageously in faith, accepting that not all will embrace the light of Christ. But Father, may we never fear rejection or persecution, knowing these are moments where we demonstrate that Your Son rules our lives. I pray that You are the only One we fear. Please present opportunities for us to reach seeking hearts and use us to show them that there is no joy in life as complete as taking up our cross and following Jesus.

THOUGHT QUESTIONS

Is the Gospel so great, and your fear and love of God so absolute, that you will stand for what is right no matter how others react?

_____

_____

With Christ ruling and the Spirit within us, what does it look like to be fearless in telling others about the Gospel and God's Power?

_____

_____

How can you start with our family? If taking up your cross and following Jesus is for every day and everywhere, how does that look in your home?

_____

_____

MATTHEW 11

John the Baptist is in prison at this point in Jesus' ministry. John sends his disciples to inquire of Jesus. This is part of John's initial intention of giving all glory and attention to the One who would come and who would be greater than him. Jesus says wonderful things about him and his ministry but powerfully adds that those who are least in the kingdom of heaven are greater than John. Sadly, many have not believed so as to realize that immense blessing. Jesus openly rebukes those who have denied the evidence, noting that many nations of old would have repented by now with such powerful proof. This saddens Jesus. He desires to call all unto Him, to lighten their heavy burdens and provide rest for their souls.

FOR MY BENEFIT

"Are you the Expected One, or shall we look for someone else?" This is a powerful question. They are asking Jesus if He is the Messiah of prophecy and John's teachings: the Savior of the world. Jesus did not simply answer yes. He spoke of His miracles and message. He had proven Himself to all who would look to Him. Many had hard hearts and would not submit, even though they had every reason to believe. Please do not let your fear, pride, and burdens keep you from repenting and turning to Jesus. Even if you are a Christian, keep renewing your gaze toward Him. He deserves and demands to lead your life. His yoke is easy, and His burden is light.

MY PRAYER

Oh wonderful God of glory, all praise to You for sending Your Son to lift our burdens. Thank You for all the incredible things He did and said during His ministry, so we can know for certain how able He is to be a Savior and Helper to us. Give us the humility to come to Him. Help us to embrace the yoke openly and earnestly that He desires to place upon us. May we learn from Him how to be loving, gentle, and humble, so that the goodness of Jesus' yoke can be shown to others.

THOUGHT QUESTIONS

Can you explain what Jesus meant when He stated that those who are least in the kingdom of heaven are greater than even John the Baptist?

_____

_____

Why do so many try to push their way into Christ's kingdom without repentance? Why is repentance so crucial to belonging to Him?

_____

_____

With all the struggles we face, how would you explain to someone that Jesus has given you rest and lightened your load in this life?

_____

_____

MATTHEW 12

The opposition of the Pharisees has been ramping up through Jesus' ministry and takes center stage in this chapter. Christ's disciples eat grain heads on the Sabbath, and the Pharisees take the opportunity to accuse them of sin. Jesus heals a man on the Sabbath, and the Pharisees conspire to destroy Him! Jesus heals a man of demonic possession, and the Pharisees accuse Him of having a demon. All along Jesus puts them in their place. His disciples violated no law by eating on the Sabbath, for Jesus is Lord of the Sabbath! It is lawful to do good on the Sabbath, including miraculously healing a lame man. Jesus works with the Spirit, not with the devil, and all who suggest such will be eternally judged for the sin of blasphemy.

FOR MY BENEFIT

Jesus goes on to say that speaking against the Spirit is worthy of eternal punishment. These evil accusations of the Pharisees indicate rotten, jealous, selfish hearts. He also exclaims that many nations of old repented on less evidence than Jesus was providing, indicating the Pharisees are far from God. We need to be humble enough to look at the Pharisees and ask, "How have I been like them?" Jesus is worthy to be worshiped, honored, and followed. We must love Him from the heart. We must love and serve His disciples as our family in the body of Christ. He defends and loves His saints. We should not be attacking or accusing others. We must be faithful supporters of one another in Christ.

MY PRAYER

Patient and Gracious God, please bear with us as we grow in our faith. Help us purge the spirit of the Pharisees in our hearts and lives. Give us wisdom to listen, to learn, and to love. And extinguish in us any desire to immediately question, judge, or attack our Lord or anyone in His family of believers. Humble us to hear His call to repentance and to respond. May the unclean spirits that flee from us by your grace not return to find a place of abode in our hearts and relationships ever again.

THOUGHT QUESTIONS

What does it mean for Jesus to tell the Pharisees, "I desire compassion and not sacrifice"? How important is compassion in evaluating others?

_____

_____

If Jesus is the Lord of the Sabbath, eternal God, and Healer of others, what place should He hold in your life today and what does that look like?

_____

_____

How important should the Christian family be to us? If we are all Jesus' "brother and sister and mother," how do you demonstrate that in service?

_____

_____

MATTHEW 13

In this packed chapter, Matthew records seven earthly stories Jesus told to make spiritual points. He begins with the parable of the Sower and the seed, which teaches the Gospel should be shared with everyone, but few will have the right heart to accept and share it. Then attention turns to the wheat and the tares, indicating that God is patient, waiting until the judgment to separate the saved and the lost. The parable of the net and fish makes this same point at the end of the chapter. Mixed in are stories about a mustard seed and pecks of flour. Two seemingly small things would grow and affect everything around them, just like Christ's kingdom! Jesus pictures His kingdom as a priceless pearl and a treasure, worth every cost to possess.

FOR MY BENEFIT

These parables are Jesus' way of helping us understand the kingdom He was coming to establish as well as the kind of people who would be in it. Many would hear the gospel and reject it, or let the world pervert it, but only a few would take it in and build their lives around it. Right now, God allows all to live on this earth, but a time is coming when He will gather His people, the faithful, and the rest will be destroyed. We must see a relationship with Jesus and His people as the greatest treasure of our lives. The kingdom started small and seemingly insignificant, but now it reaches through time and affects the entire world.

MY PRAYER

Wonderful Father, thank you for sending Jesus to teach us about His kingdom. Thank You for His parables. They give us unforgettable imagery to help us understand spiritual things. Help us to be the good soil, to take in the word, love it, and let it grow and produce. Strengthen us not to be distracted by affliction, worries, or wealth. There is no greater treasure than the kingdom of Christ. May we believe that and embrace it. Help us understand that judgment is coming, and that an eternal separation will follow. Lead us to belong to You.

THOUGHT QUESTIONS

How do you measure which kind of soil you have been lately? What is the best way to soften your heart and be more like the good soil?

If God is allowing wheat (saved) to grow with the tares (lost) until judgment, there must be a reason. What do you think that is?

What cost would you pay to possess citizenship in the kingdom of Christ? In what ways is your life demonstrating to God the truth of that claim?

MATTHEW 14

King Herod hears of Jesus' works and believes John the Baptist has risen from the dead. Sadly, John was beheaded by Herod, not many days before. Matthew records the details of that event. John was bold and faithful at the cost of his life. The rest of this chapter records Jesus' actions after hearing of this. He seeks seclusion but He is also drawn by compassion to keep healing the people. Jesus feeds the 5,000 with five loaves and two fish. Jesus then sends the disciples out in a boat, as He goes to the mountains to pray. Coming to them walking on water, He commands Peter to come out of the boat. Peter becomes frightened and Jesus asks him and all of them why they continue to doubt Him!

FOR MY BENEFIT

Jesus loved John the Baptist. He was no doubt deeply grieved by John's death. John gave his life to preach the truth, even though he opposed powerful people. This chapter reads as if Jesus has some expectation of His disciples. He is effectively saying: "My cousin just died for this cause. Is this resulting in deeper faith among My disciples?" He challenged His disciples to feed the 5,000 before doing it Himself. Jesus called Peter upon the water, before having to reach out and save him in his doubt. Jesus is looking for results. God's Son expects followers, including you and me, to grow in faith, move past doubt, and be changed by His power and His sacrifices on our behalf.

MY PRAYER

Devoted God and Father, thank you for Your willingness to endure loss for our sake. It must have been painful to watch John die, knowing that soon after Your only begotten Son would give His own life. And it must have been frustrating to see disciples still stumble in unbelief. Thank You for your patience in our weakness and thank You for continuing to demand we deepen our trust in You. Lord, help our unbelief. Train us to carry out Christ's work in faith and to walk on water through any storm, with our eyes on Jesus.

THOUGHT QUESTIONS

What kind of faith must John have had to preach morality to one who had the power to end his life? Do you and I have that kind of courage?

_____

_____

Are you comfortable with Christ expecting deeper trust from you? Why is that important for the benefit of the people in your life?

_____

_____

Would you have asked to walk to Jesus on the water? And more crucially, what does that faith look like in the storms of life today?

_____

_____

MATTHEW 15

The scribes and Pharisees are back on the scene, renewing their accusations against Jesus and His disciples, this time about the washing of hands before eating. Jesus points out how these teachers violate the actual commandments of God for the sake of their traditions. Their interpretation of the law has taken precedence over the actual teachings of God's law! Jesus reveals this is happening because of their hearts. They should be less concerned about others' dirty hands, and more concerned with their unholy hearts. This is set in contrast to the great miracles that follow. A Canaanite woman begs for healing for her daughter, and Christ commends her faith. Jesus heals many by the sea, as they glorify God. He then feeds another group of over 4,000 people, demonstrating His compassion once again.

FOR MY BENEFIT

This chapter features two very different categories of people. On the one hand, the Pharisees are supposed to be the most knowledgeable and righteous people in Israel. However, they prove to be harsh and hypocritical and ultimately miss out on the immense blessings of Christ. Set in contrast, a Gentile woman, who knows she is unworthy of Jesus, begs for His help in faith. All those who pursue Jesus are healed, fed, and blessed. We must be careful because knowledge is good, but only from pure, humble, and holy hearts. We must never let knowledge make us judges of others. May we always humbly bow before Christ, side by side, begging for His help and showing mercy to others.

MY PRAYER

Kind and Loving Father, will you seed in us Your heart of compassion and consideration of others? We thank you for the Scripture, for knowledge, and for wisdom. But Lord, we pray those things do not foster within us hearts that are hard or filled with pride. Help us to never elevate ourselves and bind things on others we have no right to bind. Open our eyes to know Your Truth, and never a truth of our own will and design. And Father, keep us humble, always placing all our expectations and hope in the grace of Your beloved Son.

THOUGHT QUESTIONS

How can you grow in knowledge without becoming like a Pharisee? Why is your heart such a powerful factor in that process?

_____

_____

Can you have convictions and "traditions" you interpret in Scripture without weaponizing them to judge others? What does this require?

_____

_____

Why is Jesus always saving and blessing people who know so little? How can you be like these people, even as you grow in knowledge?

_____

_____

Matthew 16

As Jesus begins to expand His ministry toward Jerusalem, He lays out some strong and needful teaching for His disciples. Firstly, the Pharisees and scribes are false teachers. They always seek signs because their hearts are not open to the truth. Their teachings are unkind, unlawfully binding, and must be avoided. Jesus then turns attention to "Who do people say the Son of Man is?" His point is that He is the only way, truth, and life. His church is built upon the confession of Jesus as Christ, the Son of God. He follows by explaining that the road to glory would require His suffering, death, and resurrection. The disciples struggle with this, but eternal life requires His sacrifice as well as sacrifices by all who follow Him.

FOR MY BENEFIT

There comes a time when things need to be plainly spoken. Christ was patient with the Pharisees, but it was time to warn the disciples away from their form of teaching. His church would welcome all but would only be enjoyed by those who confess Him as Christ and the Son of God. The path of faith would lead to heaven but would require extreme and total submission to God's will, perhaps even suffering or death. In the judgment, people will be willing to do anything to get to heaven, but the saved will have made that commitment during their lives here on earth. Jesus has extensively spoken to us about discipleship. Are we willing to submit and follow Him?

MY PRAYER

Great Creator and all-powerful God, teach us a form of belief that is willing to make hard choices. There are teachings around us that are false. Help us to reject them. There is a single truth that dominates the Christian: Jesus is the Christ, the Son of God. Give us the boldness to stand upon it in every part of our lives. Jesus gave everything to become our Savior. Guide us to be thankful and to put forth our lives as sacrificial offerings to You in gratitude and allegiance. Forgive our failures and strengthen us to be ready when Your Son returns.

THOUGHT QUESTIONS

The Pharisees demanded signs, even after Jesus had shown them so much. Has Christ done enough for you to be faithful to Him?

_____

_____

If the church is built upon the confession that Jesus is the Christ, the Son of God, what should that statement look like and mean in your life?

_____

_____

"For what will it profit a man if he gains the whole world and forfeits his soul? Or what will a man give in exchange for his soul?" (16:26)

_____

_____

MATTHEW 17

Jesus takes His closest three disciples on a high mountain and is transfigured right before their eyes. Peter, James, and John are amazed at Jesus' face shining like the sun. The Father then speaks and says, "This is My beloved Son, with whom I am well-pleased; listen to Him!" Following this incredible event, Matthew records something unfortunate. A boy has a demon that the disciples cannot cast out. Jesus is frustrated at their unbelief, stating this as the reason they fail to help the boy. Jesus strongly advises prayer and fasting! Faith would be crucial very soon, as Jesus again describes that He must die and be raised on the third day. The chapter ends with Jesus casually fetching poll-tax money from a fish's mouth, indicating how little such things are of concern to Him.

FOR MY BENEFIT

We have every reason to believe in the power of Christ. He is God's Son and is testified as such by the Father Himself. We must live by faith in Him. This does not mean we always understand everything about Him. The disciples had questions about what to do on the mountain and the significance of Elijah's appearance. A lack of understanding is not a lack of faith. But later, the disciples did not trust in Christ's power to cast out demons through them, and Jesus was extremely upset by their doubt. They needed more prayer and fasting to fortify their trust, especially with great trials coming. We may not always understand, but we must always believe!

MY PRAYER

Glorious Father of Light, thank You for announcing and proving the name of Jesus. By Your proclamation, and by Jesus' miracles and life, we believe! Help our unbelief, wherever it may be found. Father, will you hear our questions and continue to be patient with our lack of understanding? We pray this will not be counted as a lack of faith. But Lord, strengthen us to never doubt what Christ can do with us, around us, and through us. Help us to do great things in the name of the One who died and was raised again.

THOUGHT QUESTIONS

What would it have been like to see Jesus shine as the Father spoke of Him from heaven? What does it look like to live today as if you had seen it?

How would prayer and fasting have made all the difference in the disciples being able to cast out demons? What can those practices do for you?

If Jesus casually paid poll taxes even though He had every right not to, what does that teach us about where our focus and attention should be?

MATTHEW 18

If the previous chapter called for greater faith, then today's content serves as a potent way to develop it. The chapter opens with Jesus teaching humility to His disciples by having a child come sit on His knee. He instructs them to do whatever it takes to avoid causing such little ones to stumble. They are of tremendous value to God. Christ instructs disciples to go to great lengths to restore those who are caught in sin. Sinners should be disciplined if they continue in sin, but disciples will need forgiving hearts for restoration efforts to work. To help with this, Jesus tells a parable of a man forgiven nearly infinite debt, but who will not forgive his brother of much less. Judgment is swift upon such a one.

FOR MY BENEFIT

Growing in our trust in Jesus can be cultivated by embracing four words: humble, careful, useful, and merciful. Four sections in this chapter illuminate each one. To be like a child is to be dependent on Christ, leaning upon Him for all we need. Be humble. But we also must see our fellow believers as God's children. God will respond dramatically if we hurt His little ones. Be careful. Sometimes disciples get caught in sin and need help seeing their way out. We are called to go to them. Be useful. This means limitless forgiveness and compassion for others, as we reflect on God's patience in our lives. Be merciful. In these four ways, we honor our Savior.

MY PRAYER

Gracious Lord, we praise You for Your qualities that bring us great hope. You are humble, serving when You have the right to be served. You are careful, and patiently help us develop. You are useful, in that You never stop trying to draw us close and help us turn to You. And You are incredibly merciful and forgiving, restoring us every time we make a request. Thank You for Your incredible goodness. Today, will You help us and encourage us to demonstrate these same qualities toward others? May we do so to others to show gratitude to You.

THOUGHT QUESTIONS

What does it mean for you to be "converted and become like children"? Why do you think the kingdom requires people like this?

_____

_____

How do you balance the need to be careful with others with the command of Jesus to go show fault to a brother in sin? How can you do both?

_____

_____

Why did the man seize his neighbor who owed him little, even though he had been forgiven so much? What do we learn from this?

_____

_____

MATTHEW 19

The Pharisees again seek to test and discredit Jesus. Here they ask Him about divorce: "Is it lawful for a man to divorce his wife for any reason at all"? Jesus answers by going straight to God's word in the beginning. He then explains that the kingdom of heaven will be open to those who treasure marriage in a holy and righteous way. Following this, a rich man comes to ask about eternal life. While he is willing to keep the law, the man is not willing to give up his riches. Jesus responds by saying that it will be very hard for the rich to enter heaven. Jesus gives powerful instruction: treasure your spouse and be charitable with your money! For those who do such, they will inherit eternal life.

FOR MY BENEFIT

The greatest impact of this chapter is the dual concepts of marriage and money. Both still dominate the landscape of life today. They each have the potential to be very good for us and to honor God. But they have also been abused and twisted to dishonor God's will. Jesus' teaching on marriage goes back to the very beginning when God united a man and woman for life. May we always enter and continue in marriage with that goal in mind. Money, on the other hand, is often kept selfishly when it should be given to help others. The rich need to hear Christ's call to generosity. Those who sacrifice to honor His teachings will reap blessings now and eternally.

MY PRAYER

Wonderful Creator, give us the humility to live Your way, even when it is difficult. Your Son has beautifully answered life's most challenging questions and we pray for ears to hear. Please help us to approach marriage in a way that honors You. We pray for committed hearts, even in challenging situations, so far as it depends on us. And Lord, as rich and prosperous people, we pray for help in being generous and kingdom focused. Give us strength to trust in You, and to demonstrate that trust in our homes, with our wallets, and in every possible way.

THOUGHT QUESTIONS

How is the new law of Christ more difficult than the law of Moses? Is it easier to fight for a marriage or to divorce your spouse and leave?

What are ways you can show God's love in your marriage? And among the world, how do you show a charitable heart to others in need?

If you make great personal sacrifices to honor the will of Christ, what will be the rewards you can enjoy now, and what is coming later?

MATTHEW 20

"So the last shall be first, and the first last." Jesus explains this teaching with a parable. Workers are hired throughout the day, each agreeing to a day's wage. At the end of the day, every worker is paid the same amount. Those who were there first were angry. The point here is about God's willingness to save anyone, and our need to be humble and grateful. The disciples struggled with this at times. Later in this chapter, even after Jesus describes His coming death, the mother of James and John asks for her sons to have exalted positions. All the disciples get upset with this. Jesus informs them that the kingdom is about service, mercy, and selflessness. Jesus then demonstrates this by healing two blind men who begged for help.

FOR MY BENEFIT

Those who pridefully yearn to be first in the kingdom may miss it altogether. If Jesus had been that way, He would not have died for us, and we would be lost. The parable of the workers is designed to humble the Jews because many would later be upset by Gentiles being added to the kingdom. But it is also important for us. Maybe we are like the disciples, hoping to be rewarded for our labor. If our focus is on ourselves and what we deserve, then we miss the whole point of the kingdom. We might miss that compassion for others and service to others, even those who come after us, is what Christ and His kingdom are all about.

MY PRAYER

Kind and caring heavenly Father, thank You for being so patient with us. We sometimes get caught up in our accomplishments and our efforts and can lose sight of the fact that we are saved only by Your grace. Give us humble hearts to be grateful to be in Your vineyard and to never compare ourselves to others. Your Son died for each one of us. He took the low place to raise us up. Give us hearts and opportunities to do the same for someone in need today in honor of our humble Savior.

THOUGHT QUESTIONS

If you had worked all day, would you accept latecomers getting paid the same as you? How does this parable challenge you to check your heart?

_____

_____

What does this phrase look like in your life, your home, and your relationships: "Whoever wishes to be great among you shall be your servant"?

_____

_____

If Jesus can stop mid-mission and heal two blind men out of compassion, how might you be able to do something like that today?

_____

_____

MATTHEW 21

Jesus makes His final trip to Jerusalem before His death. He is honored and praised by many as He fulfills prophecy by riding in on a colt. Jesus goes into the temple and upsets the Jewish leaders by overturning the money tables and healing the lame and blind. The next day the leaders question Him, but they are silenced by His wisdom. He goes on to tell them two parables. The first is about two sons, one of whom said he would do good and then did not do it. This was an indictment of these chief priests and scribes. The second story is about vine growers who decide to kill the owner's son to seize his inheritance. This is a prophecy of what the Jews are planning to do to God's Son.

FOR MY BENEFIT

The contrast in this chapter is striking. So many followers worship Jesus as He enters the city. He heals many in the temple and they rejoice in Him. They believe in Him, and they will enjoy life in His kingdom. At the same time, the men in the temple are disrespecting the Father and have a fervent hatred for the Son. They question Him and seek to accuse Him. This same Jesus invokes two very different reactions. Sadly, Jesus knows they will not repent. He tells parables and quotes Scripture to indicate that the kingdom will be removed from them. Christ would be a rock of foundation for some and would crush others. They made their choice. Have you?

MY PRAYER

All powerful God, Creator, and Sustainer, thank you for sending Jesus to be our Savior and King. His message is strong and demanding. But Father, He is also the source of all grace and peace. So many in this world fight His teaching and seek to eliminate Him and seize their inheritance. Great God, may we forever forsake a life apart from Jesus. Help us to always stand upon the Rock and never be crushed by it. Father, will you lead us today to tell someone about the two paths of life and show them and teach them to choose Jesus?

THOUGHT QUESTIONS

If you were alive in Jesus' day, would you have laid your coat on the road and praised Him as He entered? How can that spirit be shown today?

_____

_____

Jesus said His disciples could move mountains "if you have faith and do not doubt." How can your prayer life show God you believe that?

_____

_____

How can you avoid a hard heart that sees the evidence but simply will not believe it? Has Jesus convinced you of His Lordship?

_____

_____

MATTHEW 22

Jesus presents the parable of the wedding feast. A king holds a banquet for his son. They invite many who are unwilling to come. Many excuses are given. The king sends armies to destroy them! He then invites people off the street until the room is filled. One man comes unprepared and is sent out. "For many will be called, but few chosen." This indicates that the kingdom requires responsiveness and faithfulness. The rest of the chapter consists of Jewish leaders trying to trap Jesus and diminish His influence. They ask about paying taxes. They ask about marriage in heaven. They question Him about the greatest law. On every occasion, He answers with integrity and righteousness. Jesus then asks them a single question about David and the Psalms, and they cannot answer Him.

FOR MY BENEFIT

Jesus' question about David was a loaded one. They knew from prophecy the Messiah would be David's son. And yet David refers to Him as Lord. How can that be? The answer is that Christ is eternal and divine. The Messiah is Jesus! We would do well to embrace that truth. Instead of questioning Him, we can learn from Him. His answers here about paying taxes, eternal life, and loving God first, are powerful truths in our lives. In the end, we must realize the Father is calling us all to the feast for His Son. We must choose to attend the feast, give proper homage to the Son, and be faithful to Him. The alternative is God's wrath.

MY PRAYER

God of limitless might, we know You will execute judgment on those who reject Your Son. You have called and invited and opened the door, and judgment is coming for all who make excuses. Lord God, help us to cast away all doubt and every temptation to turn from Your Son. Give us the wisdom to hear Him. His teachings on difficult topics like taxes and government, marriage and eternity, and loving You and others are exactly the beautiful truths You have provided for our good. Strengthen us to not just be the called, but the chosen.

THOUGHT QUESTIONS

Do you ever make excuses when called to obey God and honor His Son? Will you resolve to cast those aside and answer the invitations of God?

You may be tested by questions like the Jews did with Jesus. Are you prepared to be like Him and always answer with humility and integrity?

Do you believe Jesus when He said the greatest two commandments are to love God fully and love your neighbor? How do you show that?

MATTHEW 23

In the final week before Christ's crucifixion, He tells His disciples about the dangers of the scribes and Pharisees. After three years of patiently teaching these men, it is time to tell the world about them. Jesus first tells disciples to observe what the scribes teach if it is from God. But Christ warns them not to do what the Pharisees do. They seek to be noticed by men and to have places of honor because they lack humility. Jesus calls them hypocrites repeatedly, speaking about their lack of mercy and the underlying desire of their hearts to serve themselves. He addresses them openly and directly as "serpents"! And yet, as Jesus looks at them and all of Jerusalem, He is sorrowful that they will not repent and be gathered to Him and saved.

FOR MY BENEFIT

It is easy to read this chapter and think about other people. But it is wiser to use this list of the Pharisees' failures as a test for our own lives. In Matthew 5, Jesus told His disciples their righteousness must exceed the Pharisees if they are to be in His kingdom. These men were self-righteous. Jesus calls us to be humble servants. They were hypocritical. Jesus asks us to live out our faith. They were legalistic. We must be led to obey from a God-like heart of mercy. They were superficial. We must be honest about what's happening in our hearts. They became obstacles for others. We must live and speak to draw people to Christ.

MY PRAYER

Dear Father, we call upon Your help today, to be honest with ourselves and willing to evaluate our motives. Jesus taught so diligently to soften the hearts of the Pharisees, and they fought Him at every turn. Glorious Lord, help us to listen and to learn. May we be humble servants. Empower us to live out our faith with integrity. Build in us compassion and mercy for others. Will You create opportunities for us to help people and show them the way to Jesus? Most of all, reveal to us how much Jesus loves and yearns to save everyone.

THOUGHT QUESTIONS

Will you do the hard thing today of looking for Pharisaical tendencies in your own life? How can this be incredibly healthy and needful?

How would you define "legalism"? Can you see how some focus so intensely on the letter of the law that they miss the love that encircles it?

What does it feel like to realize that Jesus is always yearning to gather you to Him, no matter what you have done? How will you respond?

MATTHEW 24

The temple in Jerusalem was the religious center of the Jewish faith. When Jesus walks out of it and states that it will be destroyed, this brings immediate questions from His disciples. He explains that the destruction is coming, but that there will be a lot of false claims and confusion about when and how it will happen. When He came in judgment on Jerusalem, which happened by Rome's attack in 70 A.D., the believers knew to flee the city and escape desolation. It was important for Christians not to get distracted by false claims, and to stay ready to go. Jesus tells a parable about the difference between being prepared and being lazy. For them, it meant life and death. This will also be true in the final judgment on the last day.

FOR MY BENEFIT

It is debated among believers how much of this chapter is about Jerusalem's first-century destruction and how much of it points to the final day of Christ's coming. Verse 34 serves as an important guide: "...this generation will not pass away until all these things take place." It is likely that all that comes before that verse pertains to judgment on Jerusalem and the need to be wise and prepared. But the later teachings: "Be ready; for the Son of Man is coming at an hour when you do not think He will" stands as powerful instruction for us today. If we think it will not happen soon, we can lose focus and become negligent. Always be ready for Jesus!

MY PRAYER

Loving, gracious, patient Father, thank you for bearing with us in our struggles and our efforts to grow in faith. If you lacked mercy, we would have all been destroyed ages ago. We pray that Your love will produce in us the desire to be servants of You. May we build our diligent obedience to You and not be distracted by false ideas about You and Your coming. We know You alone know when the judgment day will be. Help us to build hearts of urgency, readiness, and daily expectation for the return of Your glorious Son.

THOUGHT QUESTIONS

Would you have believed Jesus if He said your city would soon be destroyed and you must be ready to leave? Do you carry that focus now?

_____

_____

Jesus expected Daniel's prophecy to be dominant in the disciples' minds. Is Christ's 1st-century promise to return a factor in your mind?

_____

_____

How do you go about getting ready and staying ready to meet the Lord? Why is it important to always expect it could be today?

_____

_____

MATTHEW 25

Jesus tells three stories to drive home one crucial point: "Be on the alert then, for you do not know the day nor the hour." Whether addressing Jerusalem's destruction or the final day, this message is needful. Whenever Christ comes in judgment, we must be prepared. The first story is about ten virgins waiting to enter a wedding feast. The groom delays and the five who brought extra oil stay ready and enter in, while the five foolish virgins run out. The second parable describes three men given talents and time to develop them. The first two immediately gain more. The third man does nothing and is unprepared when the master returns. Lastly, Jesus describes the judgment day scene. Those who serve others are saved. And those who do not are lost.

FOR MY BENEFIT

The kingdom of heaven includes a unique kind of people. While many would take enough oil to get into an important event, disciples over-prepare to make sure they can wait patiently for the Master. The world may have talents and do just enough to keep from losing them. But kingdom citizens want to use the time they have to cultivate the Father's gifts and return to Him as much profit as possible. The world may serve those who serve them and most look out for themselves. But those preparing for Christ's return will fill their lives with serving fellow believers and all people in any way they can! Jesus is showing us who He will save. We must listen carefully.

MY PRAYER

" Dear Lord, we are not worthy to be saved in the judgment. We are entirely dependent upon Your grace to be saved on the last day. But Father, we know You have called us to make a great effort to glorify You every day. Help us to get prepared and strive to stay ready. May we be driven to grow in our gifts and use the time we have to do more for You. And Father, make us servants of others. Help us remember that eternity will be decided by how we help those around us in need.

"

THOUGHT QUESTIONS

Spiritually speaking, what does it mean to have your lamp burning and extra oil with you? How do you stay that prepared to see Jesus?

_____

_____

What is a talent God has given you, and how are you presently developing it? What can you do immediately to help it grow for God?

_____

_____

If eternity is determined by how you help fellow disciples in their time of need, how much time and effort should you devote to them?

_____

_____

MATTHEW 26

As the Jewish leaders plot to kill Jesus, events take place in Jerusalem between Christ and His followers. A woman anoints His head with oil for burial, though the apostles do not understand why. Judas responds by heading off to betray Jesus for thirty pieces of silver. Jesus then gathers with the twelve at the Passover and institutes His memorial supper. He points out that He knows the betrayer. Afterward, Jesus goes to the garden to spend time in prayer and is then arrested and put before a corrupt Jewish council. At the same time, the chapter tracks Peter's journey and faith crisis from dismissing that he would ever reject Jesus, to sleeping in the garden while Jesus prayed, to ultimately denying Jesus openly after His arrest.

FOR MY BENEFIT

It is valuable to focus on the three main characters. First, there is Jesus. He is preparing His disciples for what is coming. He is leaning upon God in prayer as death approaches. He is faithful in times of trial. Jesus is the one none of us can be. Second, there is Judas. Beneath his weak faith are greed and self-focus. He shows these by trading Jesus for money, and eventually by betraying Christ to His face. He is the man we must not be. Thirdly, there is Peter. He battles pride and ignorance. But his heart is good, and he is crushed by his failure. Soon Christ will help him rebuild stronger than ever. He is an example for us all.

MY PRAYER

Loving Father, thank You for submitting Your Son to death to give us restoration and life. It is difficult to see those closest to Jesus fail Him in unbelief. But it is powerful to witness Him give His life in hopes that His sacrifice and resurrection would fortify faith and change lives. Father may that be our story. We fail. And we call upon Your mercy. Help us to be like Peter in our failings: crushed and seeking Christ's help to grow stronger. We will be humble and attentive this week to glorify Him for all He endured for us.

THOUGHT QUESTIONS

Jesus said the woman who anointed Him would always be remembered. Why? And how can you be more like her in your relationship with Jesus?

If greed was seeded in Judas's heart, someone who traveled with Jesus, how vital is it to check your heart and address worldliness?

Peter was overconfident and underprepared. He remedied this after Christ was raised. How can you learn from him and be stronger in Christ?

MATTHEW 27

Jesus is taken to Pilate, the Roman governor who sees no guilt in Him. Even Pilate's wife has a dream about His innocence. But the Jewish crowd is insistent that Jesus be crucified. One criminal is to be released, and they choose to release a murderer, Barabbas, instead of Christ. Jesus is mocked, beaten, and crucified between two criminals. When Judas sees all this taking place, he throws away the money he received and runs off to hang himself. After six hours of suffering, Jesus dies on the cross. At that moment the veil of the temple is ripped in two, and the earth quakes. A centurion remarks: "Truly this was the Son of God!" A rich man named Joseph asks for the body and buries Jesus in a new tomb.

FOR MY BENEFIT

This is the darkest moment in human history. The Jewish people put to death the very Messiah for which they had been waiting. They were angry and adamant and said, "His blood shall be on us and our children!" He was their Creator, their Savior, and the entire purpose of their law, and their envy and pride had blinded them to the truth. In all of this, Jesus was silent before His murderers. He knew His blood had to be shed to bring about a new covenant and cleansing to the world. We must never let pride blind us to the worthiness of Jesus. And we must always be grateful He was willing to endure suffering and death for our redemption.

MY PRAYER

Gracious Lord, it is shameful the way Your Son was treated and put to death by sinful men. It is sorrowful to realize that we too are sinners, and because of our sins, He had to die. Please forgive us of sins against You and against our Savior. Help us to be thankful for His sacrifice and live to honor it. As the earth shook at His death, we know the earth will shake again at His return. May we not wait until then to proclaim Him as Your Son. We will do so now and forever.

THOUGHT QUESTIONS

Have you ever felt despair like Judas, having sinned against Jesus? How is it vital to respond like Peter in those moments and not like Judas?

_____

_____

Why are envy and greed so powerful and dangerous? Are you willing to give Jesus total control of your life, or do you guard it jealously?

_____

_____

Joseph showed great courage in requesting the body of Jesus. Can you find a moment today to be the one who steps up on Jesus' behalf?

_____

_____

MATTHEW 28

This is the brightest moment in human history. Women approach the tomb early Sunday morning, and the stone is rolled away. An angel appears to them and says the most triumphant thing about Jesus: "He is not here, for He has risen, just as He said." Jesus then appears to the women, and they are amazed and worship Him. He sends them to the disciples to report the news. At the same time, the guards report what happened, but they are paid to lie and say the body was stolen. That story spreads in their day, though Matthew exposes it in this letter. The eleven disciples go to Galilee to meet Him. They see Jesus and worship Him. Jesus tells them to proclaim His authority and to preach baptism and faithfulness.

FOR MY BENEFIT

The four Gospels add different elements to Christ's resurrection story. Matthew's account focuses heavily on proof that Jesus is risen. The first report comes from a shining angel. Then Jesus Himself appears to the women. Any attempt to cover this up is false and hollow. He met with the apostles and told them exactly what to share with others. This means we can put full confidence in their teachings in the book of Acts and the epistles. Matthew's testimony is substantiated by multiple witnesses. The tomb was empty and will always be empty. Jesus is risen and ruling. We must observe all He has commanded us, and He will be with us until the end of the age.

MY PRAYER

Great Lord, with Your victorious and exalted Son, all glory be given to You and to Christ. Your Son defeated our greatest enemies: Satan, sin, and death. No grave could hold Him, no lies could diminish Him, and no force of darkness could stop Him. He is our King, and we love Him. Father, guide us and help us understand what that means. All authority over our lives belongs to Him. We seek to love Him, obey Him, and live in full confidence that He is with us. Help us develop a faith that will live in His honor today.

THOUGHT QUESTIONS

Why do you believe that Jesus Christ was raised from the dead? And how is your life different because your King defeated death?

_____

_____

The women saw Jesus and bowed down to worship Him. You would have done the same. How are you bowing before Him in your life?

_____

_____

Will you allow Jesus to rule your life? Have you been baptized? If that is His command, will you submit to Him and obey His will today?

_____

_____

MARK 1

Mark's gospel is the shortest of the four and packs lots of information in each chapter. For instance, this opening chapter begins with John the Baptist preaching and Jesus coming to him to be baptized. Immediately following this, Jesus is led by the Spirit into the wilderness and tempted by Satan. The text moves to Jesus selecting His first four followers: Peter, Andrew, James, and John. The rest of the chapter documents miracles and Jesus' works in Galilee: casting out a demon, healing Peter's mother-in-law, moved by compassion to heal a leper, as well as references to other miraculous works. Mark is interested in getting to Jesus' ministry quickly and spending a great deal of time there. The word "immediately" is used throughout, as the stories move at a rapid pace.

FOR MY BENEFIT

The key to applying fuller chapters is to find the theme or thread. In today's reading, the words about Jesus tie the events together. John the Baptist said, "After me One is coming who is mightier than I..." The Father said, "You are My beloved Son, in You I am well pleased." Even the demon said, "I know who You are – the Holy One of God!" God, men, and even demons know who Jesus is. Do we? Following this testimony, more proofs are seen in His miracles. Jesus, filled with compassion, heals a leper who pleads for help. Though instructed to stay quiet, the leper demonstrates thankfulness by sharing the glory of Jesus with everyone. We should do the same!

MY PRAYER

Kind Father, who spoke for ages about the coming of Your Son, praise be to You for sending Him to be our Healer and Savior. He came to live in the flesh, subjected Himself to Your will, refused the devil's temptations, and devoted His life to teaching and helping others. Help us to love Him as He deserves to be loved. May we see His miracles and know who He is and what He can do. Like the leper pleading for help, may Jesus see us and be moved with compassion to make us clean and new in Him.

THOUGHT QUESTIONS

If John the Baptist, God from heaven, and even demons confessed the name of Jesus, should you be doing so openly and boldly?

_____

_____

The disciples "immediately" left their nets to follow Jesus. That word connotes urgency. In what ways should your faith involve urgency?

_____

_____

The leper, once healed, was told not to speak of Jesus, but he too pro-claimed Him openly. What has Jesus done for you that must be shared?

_____

_____

MARK 2

This chapter strings together events that seem unrelated, but they all have something in common: Jewish accusers. Jesus heals the paralytic who is lowered down to Him through a roof by his friends. The scribes quickly accuse Jesus of blasphemy for forgiving the lame man's sins. Following this, Jesus calls Matthew, a tax collector, to follow Him. A dinner is held at Matthew's house and many sinners are invited to see Jesus. The Pharisees stand outside and accuse Jesus of ungodly behavior. After a brief conversation with John the Baptist's disciples, Jesus and His disciples pass through a grain field. The disciples eat from the field, and the Pharisees show up and accuse them of violating the Law. Jesus silences them with these words: "The Son of Man is Lord even of the Sabbath."

FOR MY BENEFIT

Amid the Pharisees' fault-finding mission is a series of beautiful moments with Jesus. The lame man had friends willing to work to get him to Jesus, resulting in Jesus rewarding their faith with forgiveness of sins. Matthew is called to Christ and organizes a dinner so that others may know Him. Jesus is willing and says, "I did not come to call the righteous, but the sinners." This is a time of celebration, as He points out to John's followers. We live in a time like this, amplified by the resurrection of Jesus. He heals and forgives and seeks to save sinners. Surround yourself with friends who pull you nearer to Him. And be that friend for someone else.

MY PRAYER

Omnipotent Father, no one can stand against You or Your Son. The Pharisees failed every time to discredit Him, as unbelievers do today. Lord God, soften their hearts to know the Savior. We pray to hear Him through all the noise and understand that all help and healing are found when we are closer to Him. Help us be wise in choosing people in our lives who help us draw near to Jesus. And Father, create opportunities for us to bring others to Him. Use us bountifully during this time of feasting and joy in Jesus.

THOUGHT QUESTIONS

The Pharisees asked, "Who can forgive sins but God alone?" A great question. Do you understand that Jesus is God and can forgive your sins?

_____

_____

If Jesus came to call sinners, even those cast aside by others, did Jesus come to call you? Who else do you know who needs to hear that?

_____

_____

The Jews thought they controlled the Sabbath. But Jesus is the Lord of the Sabbath. Is Jesus also the Lord over your daily life and worship?

_____

_____

MARK 3

Christ's early ministry continues as the Pharisees resume their accusations. Jesus heals a lame man in the synagogue on the Sabbath day. He points out the anger residing in the hearts of the Jewish leaders. They respond by conspiring against Him. Jesus withdraws to the sea and casts out many unclean spirits. Unlike the scribes, the demons proclaim, "You are the Son of God!" Before returning to Capernaum, Jesus chooses His twelve apostles. They return to the city where the scribes are waiting once again. They argue that Jesus casts out demons by the power of the devil! This is how deluded and hateful the unbelieving heart can get. He warns them that the Holy Spirit is the power behind the miracles and that blasphemy against Him would be eternal sin.

FOR MY BENEFIT

The Pharisees lacked mercy, even as Jesus demonstrated so much grace around them. A man had his hand restored in the synagogue. Many were healed of infirmities and had evil spirits driven away from them. How wonderful must that have been? The twelve were chosen and would soon have the power to proclaim Christ through the power of the Holy Spirit. That must have been amazing. The scribes, however, rejected the Spirit and put their souls at eternal risk. The chapter ends with Jesus calling all who do the will of God His family. We can be helped and protected in His family. May we never harden our hearts and miss out on these blessings in Christ!

MY PRAYER

Great God of heaven, You are worthy of all praise and adoration. Your Son has all power and wisdom and glory, on earth and in heaven. Strengthen us to trust Him and love Him more each day. May we never limit what He can do or question His authority. Guide us to believe in His Holy Spirit and to never blaspheme against the Spirit, the Son, or You. Jesus chose His family of faith even over His blood family. Please hold us close within that family and give us that same love for our brothers and sisters in Christ.

THOUGHT QUESTIONS

The Jews had no compassion for people, lame or otherwise. Is there a risk that your beliefs could lead to a lack of love and attention for others?

_____

_____

Do you have to understand everything about the Holy Spirit to trust in His power? How do you keep from blasphemy against the Spirit?

_____

_____

What does it mean for you to be in the family of God? How should that inspire obedience to the Father and time with your brothers and sisters?

_____

_____

MARK 4

Jesus addresses His followers. He shares the parable of the sower and the seed. The seed is spread in all directions. It falls on four surfaces: the road, rocky ground, among the thorns, and into the good soil. The seed fails to grow in the first three soils but prospers in the good soil. Jesus later explains the soils represent different hearts. Only one of the four would befit the kingdom. Jesus adds two more parables that teach that growth is possible in swift and powerful ways: the overnight sprout and the large mustard plant. An event at sea tests the personal spiritual growth of the disciples. A great storm comes up and their faith falters. Jesus expects them to grow in faith and eliminate the fear that holds them back.

FOR MY BENEFIT

Jesus uses parables to challenge the hearer. If we have a heart for Him, these stories transform our lives. If we are not seeking truth, they have little impact. The parable of the sower reinforced Jesus' teaching: "Many will be called, but few will be chosen." Some will not listen. Some will hear and then be overcome with fear. Some will hear but let worry and greed rule their lives. The seed, the Word of God, is perfect and powerful and can completely transform us. But we must open our hearts, put aside all else, and receive His word deep within us. Even then, faith will be tested by the elements, by storms, and by trials. We must trust in Jesus.

MY PRAYER

Dear Father, Your grace and love for mankind are abundantly clear in the coming of Jesus. Thank You for sharing the life-giving word with all the world. It is sad to think how many reject Your word or let fear and temptation rob it from their hearts. Please soften hearts in this world and use us to share the life-changing Gospel. And Father, please help the truth to sink more deeply into us as well. May we bear fruit for you, face our fears, and stand strong with trust in Jesus during the trials and temptations of life.

THOUGHT QUESTIONS

What will you do today because you are striving to be the good soil? How do you keep from becoming like the rocky or thorny soil?

_____

_____

Do you believe change can happen in your heart and life? Do you believe that God can do big things through you if you let Him?

_____

_____

Are you prepared for your faith to be tested? How will you trust in Jesus when things get scary, hard, or temptation rages around you?

_____

_____

MARK 5

Three miracles of Jesus are documented in this chapter. Each is given significant detail. The first is Jesus casting demons out of a man and into a herd of swine. The man is in torment and the demons are many, but they are subject to the authority of Christ. They even ask permission from Jesus to be cast into the pigs. The second miracle is with a woman who has been bleeding for twelve years. Amid a massive crowd, she pushes through and touches His coat and is immediately healed. Jesus praises her faith. The final miracle is raising a synagogue official's daughter from the dead! Jesus tells the man, "Do not be afraid any longer, only believe." Peter, James, and John are allowed to witness this incredible miracle!

FOR MY BENEFIT

Each of these stories tells us something about Jesus' authority. Casting out the demons shows that Jesus controls all the spiritual realms. The demons knew He was "the Son of the Most High God," and they were powerless against Him. The woman's healing demonstrates Jesus' power over the human body, as He heals her in an instant. The raising of Jairus's daughter proves Jesus can bring life after death. All of this is designed to increase our faith. He controls the demons and casts them away from us. He can heal and protect and help us and our bodies. And not even death can separate us from the power of Jesus, who commands our souls to come and go wherever He chooses.

MY PRAYER

> *Great God of glory, we believe in the authority and power of Your Son Jesus Christ. We believe He controls the spiritual world beyond our sight. We know He has power over our bodies and lives. And we live with the assurance that He has the keys to death and hades and will give us life again after physical death. He has proven His ability in the miracles of His ministry and His resurrection from the dead. Please empower us to remember and share these eternal truths. Help us to surrender our lives to His authority.*

THOUGHT QUESTIONS

The man with the demon needed Jesus. You may be overcome by struggles you cannot bear alone. How should you approach Jesus about those?

_____

_____

The woman was desperate when she reached for Jesus' cloak. Have you ever felt like that? And what does it look like to reach out for Him?

_____

_____

The people laughed when Jesus said He would raise the girl. Do you believe Jesus will raise you? How does that affect your daily life?

_____

_____

MARK 6

Jesus returns to His hometown but is not greatly honored there. He does few miracles because of their unbelief. He then summons the twelve apostles and sends them out in pairs to work miracles and teach people to repent of their sins. They have wonderful success in the ministry. Following this, Jesus works two large-scale miracles: He feeds the 5,000 followers with five loaves and two fish. And after sending the disciples across the sea in a boat, He approaches them walking on the water! The disciples are astonished because their hearts are not yet fully softened to understanding the glory of Christ. Between these events, the author Mark records the story of John the Baptist being beheaded by Herod at the request of the daughter of Herodias.

FOR MY BENEFIT

This chapter shows the challenges Jesus faced in His ministry. He was the perfect Teacher, and yet people in His hometown doubted Him. He sent out the apostles and they did well, but at other times they didn't understand His power to feed the people or control the water on the sea. Added to this, Jesus' cousin John the Baptist died at the hands of evil men, and this brought Jesus great sorrow. Two lessons emerge. First, Jesus never gave up. He stayed patient and committed and kept going and teaching. Two, we must carry His spirit into our daily walk. Some will doubt us, while others support us. Some may leave us. We must keep going in Christ.

MY PRAYER

" *God of patience and grace, it is hard to imagine people seeing Your Son in the flesh and doubting His worthiness. And yet, He faced an assortment of doubters and disappointments. We praise Him for His endurance and limitless love for people. Thank you for feeding us and calming the seas, even when we do not have the depth of faith that we should. May Your Son's work in our lives open our eyes to His nearness and give us the courage to live each day in confidence. And please send us out on the mission of sharing His great name!* "

THOUGHT QUESTIONS

If Jesus received less honor in His hometown, what can you expect from the people who have known you the longest? How will you react to that?

_____

_____

John the Baptist lost his life in service to God. How does his story give you the resolve to be strong in truth even when others do not approve?

_____

_____

Jesus was not always pleased with His disciples, but He never stopped mentoring them. Do you believe He has that same patience with you?

_____

_____

MARK 7

The Pharisees show up making accusations against Jesus' disciples for not properly washing their hands. Jesus quickly confronts them about enforcing their traditions on others, while at the same time, neglecting actual commandments! Jesus then explains to His disciples that these accusations are matters of the heart. If the intentions of the heart are selfish, prideful, and bitter, then it will show up in a merciless view and application of God's law. Following the educated Pharisee's sinfulness, we are introduced to a Gentile woman who pleads for Jesus' help to cure her demon-possessed daughter. She begs for His help, and He rewards her faith. Jesus also heals a deaf man. The leaders who know the law are condemned, and those who do not know it well, but have humble hearts, are blessed!

FOR MY BENEFIT

The contrast between the characters in this chapter is potent. It opens with the Jewish leaders accusing, being unkind, and enforcing their own rules. They neglected important laws of mercy, like caring for their parents. In comparison, the Gentile woman is utterly humble before the Lord so that she can save her daughter! She is entirely motivated by love and unrelenting in her pursuit of Jesus. We must be constantly checking our hearts, especially as we grow in knowledge. We will never be any more worthy than the Gentile woman or the deaf man. We must approach Jesus for help and be willing to carry His spirit of compassion to everyone around us, including our parents.

MY PRAYER

❝ Dear Lord, we call upon You to examine our hearts. Your Son teaches that the intentions of the heart represent the true nature of a person. Cleanse us of all pride, evil thoughts, deceit, and ungodly anger. Help us understand how to know Your law and teach it, but with a spirit of kindness, patience, and love. May we never be as foolish and misguided as the Pharisees. Instead, teach us to be like the Gentile woman and the deaf man, who humbly pursued Jesus. We call upon Him for blessings in our lives and for those we love. ❞

THOUGHT QUESTIONS

Knowledge can lead to pride. How are you careful not to bind your interpretations of Scriptures on others unlawfully as the Pharisees did?

How do you check your heart? Jesus says that is the key to everything. What is the process of making sure your heart is pure and undefiled?

A man prayed for his ears to be cleared and His tongue mended. In a spiritual sense, how can you pray for similar things today?

MARK 8

Jesus has a compassionate heart. This leads him to feed thousands because He sees that they are hungry. This is a sign of His power and love. However, the Pharisees come asking for more signs. For them, nothing Jesus does will be enough to believe. It is this hard-heartedness He warns the disciples to avoid. Jesus then heals a blind man. This physical sight given by faith is set in contrast to the Pharisees who think they see and yet remain spiritually blind. Jesus then asks His disciples who they believe Him to be. They say, "You are the Christ." This faith would be crucial, as their faith would be tested by His arrest and death, as well as the extreme sacrifices they would be called to make in His name.

FOR MY BENEFIT

Jesus demonstrates His glory and His right to be called the Christ. We must choose whether to believe in Him or not. But this cannot be done halfway. His call to disciples is extreme. It starts with demanding we understand that His Lordship would require His death. Peter struggled with this. More than that, He demands allegiance from us for His glory. We must deny ourselves, take up our crosses, and follow Him. We must lose our life in devotion to Him to see the salvation of our lives in eternity. Many will want to give everything to be saved in the judgment and will have nothing to give. We must serve Him now, confessing His name courageously in this world.

MY PRAYER

Great Father, we thank You for your lovingkindness and the compassion that Your Son has for us. We know that His ability to help us is only limited by the borders of our faith. Help us to expand our trust and surrender our entire lives to Him. We sometimes fall into pride, blindness to truth, and even doubts about Your will. But great God, we believe Your Son is the Christ sent to die for our salvation. Forgive our failings and restore us to commitment and strength and to never be ashamed of our Lord.

THOUGHT QUESTIONS

Do you believe Jesus sees you and feels for you in times of struggle? How do you trust in that, even when results do not come right away?

_____

_____

The Pharisees had things in their hearts that blinded them to Christ's glory. What has He done in your life to keep your heart from hardening?

_____

_____

What does it mean to lose your life for His sake? And what would it profit you to keep your life and gain the world but not have Jesus?

_____

_____

MARK 9

Jesus is transfigured on the mountain, as Peter, James, and John look on. They see Elijah and Moses appear, and they hear the Father say: "This is My beloved Son, listen to Him!" This is a great moment of honor for the Son. Afterward, however, many seem to lack full trust in Him. The disciples lack the faith to cast a demon from a boy, and Jesus must step in and do it. Jesus later tries to teach the disciples more about His coming death, but they are enamored with a discussion of who among them is greatest. Jesus emphasizes the greatest to be the one who serves. He then teaches about not causing others to stumble, and instead making sacrifices to serve them. Hell is reserved for those who refuse.

FOR MY BENEFIT

The comforting part about the imperfect faith of the disciples is that we can relate. He had shown them so much. And He was counting on them to shine so brightly. Yet, they sometimes were not prayerful enough and lacked the power to do great things. They often got sidetracked about places of honor and personal greatness. We know too well those same shortcomings and emotions. And yet, Jesus came to save us. He came to patiently teach us and help us grow in understanding. He warns us of the possibility of hell if we are prideful and hurt others, but even that warning is an act of grace to help us yearn and strive for greater faith.

MY PRAYER

Holy, heavenly Father. We know You sit in a place of eternal glory. Thank You for sending Jesus to this earth to lead us home to You. Thank You for testifying of His glory in wonderful ways. We lack the faith You deserve. Lord, we believe; but we ask you to help our unbelief. Help us to make time to pray, and to commit to a closer walk with Christ. May that extend beyond just loving Him and cause us to be more loving and committed to the people You put in our lives, careful to not make them stumble.

THOUGHT QUESTIONS

The Father said, "This is My beloved Son, listen to Him!" How do those words affect you? What are some things Jesus said that you must hear?

_____

_____

Jesus was upset when the man said, "If you can do anything, take pity on us." How does faith require more than just asking "if" Jesus can help?

_____

_____

To cause tender souls to stumble is highly offensive to the Lord. How far are you willing to go to keep someone from being discouraged?

_____

_____

MARK 10

This chapter is packed with events: the Pharisees question Jesus about divorce and the rich young ruler turns from Jesus when asked to sell all he has. Jesus speaks of how difficult it is for the rich to be saved. The apostles have given up everything, but they struggle to understand that the mission will cost Jesus His life and theirs as well. James and John ask for positions of glory, but Jesus informs them that great sacrifice will be required first. A blind beggar approaches asking Jesus to heal Him. The disciples try to silence him, but Jesus heals him because of his faith. There is a common thread of love and mercy throughout all these stories. Everyone needs to learn that the kingdom is about caring for others.

FOR MY BENEFIT

The Pharisees asked about divorce. But that was not God's will, because it would be unloving and consequential for the wife who was sent away. The rich man was asked to sell his goods and give them to help the poor, but he did not have the heart to do it. The apostles sought places of honor because they struggled to see the mission as being about others. They even tried to prevent a blind man from being healed. Jesus came to earth because He loves us and wants to provide blessings for us. His followers will make decisions based on how they will benefit other people. We are here to love God and our neighbor with sacrificial love.

MY PRAYER

" *Wonderful Father of love, please soften our hearts to feel more love and compassion for others. It was Your love for us that brought Your Son to come and die for our sins. Whether it is our spouse, the poor among us, or fellow brothers and sisters in Christ, help us to make decisions that reflect care for them. Selfishness is dangerous and hurtful. Cleanse our hearts and make us more like Your Son. Give us the wisdom to see the blind around us looking for sight and develop in us the Christ-like compassion to show Jesus to them.* "

THOUGHT QUESTIONS

What would happen to divorce in our country if everyone prioritized selfless love and service for the person they chose to marry?

_____

_____

How would the poor and homeless be affected in our area if all believers extended charity to them in the likeness of Jesus' kindness to us?

_____

_____

Will you take some time today to look around at people, all people, and see them with the same love and compassion that Jesus does?

_____

_____

MARK 11

The events of this chapter connect to a barren fig tree. Jesus approaches a tree that has no fruit on it. He immediately condemns it to never bear figs again. The next day, the tree is shriveled up and the disciples ask about it. Jesus responds with these four words: "Have faith in God." He goes on to say that incredible things are possible if disciples trust in God. In Jesus' midst are people of faith, like those who lay down coats and worship Jesus as He enters Jerusalem. But there are also hard-hearted Pharisees who have no faith. They defile God's temple with money tables. And they question Christ's authority over them, though He silences them almost immediately. They are like that fig tree, condemned for being spiritually barren.

FOR MY BENEFIT

The gospel of Jesus has had the same effect, all over the world, for centuries. Some believe. They lay their coats before Him and worship Him as their King. Believers pray in His name, live with great faith, and bear amazing fruit in His honor. These are the few and they belong to Him. But there are always many who live for themselves, are overtaken by greed, and will not submit to Christ's right to rule their lives. They are plants with every ability to thrive but are fruitless and dead. We must choose, every day, which of the two we are going to be. We are the fig trees, and Jesus has the ongoing right to draw from us richly.

MY PRAYER

Loving Father and gift giver, we praise Your name for the coming of Jesus to be our Savior and King. May we sing as believers did when He entered Jerusalem: "Hosanna! Blessed is He who comes in the name of the Lord..." Indeed He is blessed, and He is a blessing to all who believe in Him. Help us to bear fruit by His power and for His glory. Lead us to be prayerful, to ask forgiveness when our branches grow bare, and to give Him the authority and the right to draw from us things that please Him.

THOUGHT QUESTIONS

The plant imagery is helpful. If you are a fig tree that belongs to Jesus, how does that impact the nourishment and growth you pursue daily?

Jesus was deeply offended that the temple of God was infiltrated by greed. Is there a sense in which that has meaning for us in His church?

There is instruction on prayer in this chapter. Why does Jesus call us to forgive "anything against anyone" before we seek God's forgiveness?

MARK 12

Jesus and the Jewish leaders battle in this chapter. It begins with the parable of the vineyard workers. They attack the owner's delegates and eventually kill his son. The result was wrath from the father and the destruction of the murderers. The Jews know Jesus is talking about them, so they send inquisitors to try and trap Jesus in His words. They ask Him about paying poll taxes to Caesar. Jesus responds by saying to give Caesar his taxes. They ask about a seven-time widow and her marriage in heaven. Jesus responds with divine wisdom about eternity. They ask about the greatest commandment, and He responds perfectly with the law of love. These prideful men are set in contrast with the humble widow who contributes all that she has to God.

FOR MY BENEFIT

The widow at the end is praised by Jesus because her devotion to God is real and sacrificial. She is fully committed to God, while many others only give out of their surplus. She is the opposite of the Jewish leaders. The parable at the beginning is about killing the son of the owner so they can have the vineyard. The motivation is selfishness and greed. All their questions for Jesus are about diminishing Him so they don't have to submit. Their main priority is themselves and what they can get and keep. We are challenged to be less like them and more like the widow at the end. It cannot be about us and Him. We must choose Him.

MY PRAYER

Benevolent Father, You are a gracious gift giver and we have all that we could ever need. Help us to see this in Jesus and His church and to flee the temptation to be greedy and worldly. The Pharisees turned against Jesus because He sought a seat of authority in their hearts that they wanted for themselves. Father, forgive our selfish thinking and any greed or envy that is born of it. Train us to trust Jesus and never to question His wisdom. Humble us to be like the widow, freely giving all that we have to You.

THOUGHT QUESTIONS

How does your life change when you see yourself as belonging to God, instead of seeing God and His creation as merely gifts for you?

_____

_____

The Jews asked hard questions of Jesus. We may ask some as well. What is the right way to approach your King when asking for clarity?

_____

_____

Most believers are somewhere between the ones giving out of surplus and the widow giving all she had. How do we grow in this area?

_____

_____

MARK 13

Jesus leaves the temple and announces that it will be completely torn down. His four closest apostles later ask Him about this devastating event. Jesus tells them that many things must happen first, and they should not believe those who claim to know the time of the temple's destruction. The gospel must first be preached. The apostles would face heavy persecution before it happened. But when the attack draws near, He warns them to flee to the mountains and get far away from Jerusalem. It will be a judgment on the Jews and the destruction will be accomplished by Jesus. These things would happen during their generation. The disciples are warned not to be misled by false teachers, but to stay alert. No one knows the day or the hour.

FOR MY BENEFIT

Jesus describes the destruction of Jerusalem. It was the judgment of Christ after He ascended to heaven, but it was carried out by the Roman government. Jerusalem was destroyed, many Jews were killed, and the temple was completely dismantled. This was God's punishment upon the Jews for killing His Son and refusing His kingdom. This took place in 70 A.D. Leading up to it, there were rumors and false prophecies. Jesus was warning about that decades in advance. The key was to stay alert and ready to go. This has clear parallels to the destruction that is coming in the final judgment and our need to be alert and prepared. No one knows the day or the hour.

MY PRAYER

Dear Father, we know You took no joy in the destruction of the Jewish city, temple, and people. Your judgment was forced by their refusal to honor Christ. They were warned, and most did not listen. Great God, we pray for open hearts and ears. Help us to commit to Christ and to wait for His return. Sadly, it will also be a judgment day against the ungodly, and it will come on a day no one knows. We want to be ready. Please discipline us to be on the alert, so we will be saved when that day comes.

THOUGHT QUESTIONS

God destroyed His temple because of unbelief among the Jews. What does that tell you about how serious the Father is about faithful living?

Before the judgment day of God, the apostles would have to face persecution and trust in the Spirit. Are you prepared to do the same today?

There is a final day of judgment coming. What are the daily things you think and do to make sure you are always prepared for His return?

MARK 14

Mark's gospel moves swiftly toward Jesus' arrest and trial. There is a powerful contrast between the woman who anoints Him with expensive oil and Judas who betrays Him for thirty pieces of silver. Both would be remembered for generations for very different reasons. Jesus proceeds to meet with the disciples and institute the memorial supper. He announces that a betrayer would come from among them. But He later tells them that, in the short term, they will all fall away. Peter, of course, denies this vehemently. Following this, Jesus prays in the garden, while Peter, James, and John fall asleep a short distance away. Jesus is then arrested and accused of blasphemy by Jewish leadership. In those moments, Peter falters in faith and denies Jesus three times. Peter then weeps in sorrow.

FOR MY BENEFIT

The potency of this chapter is in the characters around Jesus. The woman anoints Him with costly oil, demonstrating service and her understanding of His sacrifice. Judas, on the other hand, lets greed dominate his thinking. It has blinded him to true and selfless faith. We would do well to study them both and decide who we want to emulate. The rest of the chapter turns attention to Peter and his pride. He said he would never desert Jesus. While he certainly had a stronger faith than Judas, he did not prepare well to stand firm. He was overconfident and it cost him. We should learn humility from this story, to pray fervently, and to prepare for temptation.

MY PRAYER

Dear loving Father, who sent Your Son to die for our sins and redeem us to You. Thank You for His willingness to suffer and die for us. Some never understood the value of His death. Some even contributed to it. Others struggled to understand what it means to stand up for it. Lord God, help us to learn from all those people. Give us the gratitude to praise His sacrifice every day and help us develop the humility to spend time each day in prayer. Prepare us and encourage us to share in His suffering with selfless, faithful living.

THOUGHT QUESTIONS

Judas traveled with Jesus but harbored greed in his heart. How do you cultivate your heart to remain selfless and free from greed?

The Lord's Supper is important to Jesus and to Christians. How are you already preparing to partake on Sunday in fellowship with Jesus?

Peter was a man of faith, but he had a lot to learn about humility, prayer, and facing temptation. What do you learn from his example?

MARK 15

Mark's record of Christ's crucifixion focuses heavily on the people around Him. The Jewish leaders seek to kill him. Pilate gives in to them, but he is confused about the Christ. Barabbas, an actual murderer, is released instead of Jesus. Soldiers scourge the Messiah, beat Him, mock Him, and crucify Him. Jewish onlookers relentlessly attack Him. The two criminals hurl abuse at Him. But at His death, the focus shifts to people of faith. The Centurion says, "Truly this man was the Son of God!" Women of faith stay close to the body of Jesus. Joseph of Arimathea requests the body and gives Him a proper burial. This sets a contrast between the sinful work of man in Christ's death and the faith and hope that would grow from His sacrifice.

FOR MY BENEFIT

The sinful work of man is on full display during Jesus' trial and crucifixion. People get so sure of what they believe, and they let envy and pride lead them to the most heinous behavior. We must learn from their failures. We must check our hearts, pride, and intentions, to center them on honoring Christ. If not, we may end up living our lives against Him. If we trust in Him, then His life, death, and resurrection can become the anthem of our lives. So many have been changed by His sacrifice, like the Centurion and Joseph in our story. That change is possible in you. But also, in many around us, if we will share Jesus with them.

MY PRAYER

" *Tender Father, how painful it must have been to watch Your Son be ridiculed by those He came to save. Above all today, we pray to never be that way in Your sight. Humble and mold us to be people who appreciate His death and who seek to glorify Him because of His sacrifice. Lord God, give us a voice to proclaim the Gospel message. Others are living in sin and need to see what He did and learn to love Him for it. Will you reveal those people to us today and give us the courage to speak His name?* "

THOUGHT QUESTIONS

Pilate is a tragic character. He was conflicted about Jesus, but he ultimately relented. How does your faith show more resolve than Pilate?

_____

_____

Jesus' death changed people, like the criminal and the Centurion. Do you think His self-sacrifice still has the power to do that today?

_____

_____

The women and Joseph were faithful even at personal risk. How does your life prove that you serve Jesus no matter what cost is required?

_____

_____

MARK 16

Women followers of Jesus come to the tomb early on Sunday morning, hoping to anoint His body with spices. They arrive to see the stone rolled away. A young man is sitting inside the tomb, an angel of the Lord, who tells them the most wonderful thing about Jesus: "He has risen." Jesus then appears to Mary Magdalene and sends her to report to the disciples. When they hear, they refuse to believe. Jesus appears to two other disciples. They report it to the apostles, who still will not believe. Jesus then comes to the eleven and reproaches them for their unbelief. He charges them to go and preach the Gospel to all, performing miracles to confirm His word. They witness Jesus ascend into heaven and immediately begin spreading His message.

FOR MY BENEFIT

The empty tomb is the most life-changing event of all time. It took some time for the disciples to believe it, as they had always struggled to understand the death portion of Jesus' ministry. But His resurrected appearance in the flesh changed all of that. The followers of Christ went from fear to faith, committing themselves to sharing the power of Jesus over death. Having watched Him ascend into heaven, they gave their lives teaching others that He would once again return. If we believe in His resurrection, then our hopes are forever secure, our fear is taken away, and we can live for Jesus in full assurance of faith, sharing His message everywhere and with everyone.

MY PRAYER

Great Father of Power, we believe. We believe that the grave is empty. We believe Jesus has forever defeated Satan, sin, and death. Thank You for the testimony of eyewitnesses and all the evidence of His resurrection. Please provide us opportunities to share this message with others and open their hearts to move from fear to faith, from unbelief to absolute assurance. Father, we are committed to the ministry charged to believers. Please help us to be so certain of Christ's ascension and return that we will share the Gospel in any environment and with everyone we know.

THOUGHT QUESTIONS

Why do you believe Jesus was raised from the dead? How important are the proofs of His resurrection to know and share?

Christ's resurrection changed the apostles forever. How is your life changed by the death, burial, resurrection, and ascension of Jesus?

We are not apostles, but we are messengers of Christ. What can you do today to share saving belief and baptism with someone you love?

LUKE 1

Luke opens his letter by noting that he has investigated things carefully so he can report "the exact truth." He details the events surrounding the birth of John the Baptist and the conception of Jesus in the longest chapter in the New Testament. Elizabeth is barren until an angel appears to her and Zacharias and tells them they will have a son named John. Six months later, the angel Gabriel appears to Mary. He tells her she will conceive of one named Jesus, "the Son of the Most High," who will reign forever! Mary visits Elizabeth and offers a beautiful prayer of praise to God. After Mary's departure, John is born, and his father Zacharias prophesies concerning redemption, mercy, forgiveness, and peace! The age of the Savior begins!

FOR MY BENEFIT

Luke sets out on a specific mission with this Gospel. This record of the life of Jesus provides carefully researched facts intended to build the faith of a man named Theophilus, and it can do so for all who read it today. It begins by showing God's supernatural involvement in the birth of John, the forerunner for Jesus. Angels from heaven appear to Elizabeth and Mary. Elizabeth's womb is open. Zacharias is struck mute for a time. Later he regains his speech, is "filled with the Holy Spirit", and begins to prophesy. The story of Jesus begins with God's hand directly involved in the affairs of mankind. God actively accomplishes redemption for those who would see His works and believe.

MY PRAYER

Benevolent Lord, among all the gifts You have given, there are none as valuable as Your Son. We praise You for Gabriel's message to Mary, that Jesus would rule and "His kingdom would have no end." Living in that kingdom is our daily and constant source of peace. We see Your consistency and wisdom in bringing John the Baptist into the world to fulfill prophecy and prepare the way for Jesus. His teachings call people to repent and surrender their lives to Christ. Lord help us to receive that message and prepare ourselves to be led by the Savior.

THOUGHT QUESTIONS

Elizabeth and Zacharias were "both righteous in the sight of God" and they were blessed. Does God hear and help people of faith today?

_____

_____

Zacharias questioned the angel's words and was struck mute for nine months. Might God still react like that if we doubt His promises?

_____

_____

Mary praised God, believing she carried the Messiah. Why is it important to rejoice in faith even before we see incredible outcomes?

_____

_____

LUKE 2

Joseph and Mary travel to Bethlehem for a census. Jesus is born there in a manger since the inn is full. An angel appears to shepherds proclaiming Jesus as the "Savior, who is Christ the Lord." A multitude of angels then appear praising God! The shepherds visit the family and report these wonderful things. After eight days, Jesus' family takes Him to Jerusalem to present Him to the Lord at the temple. A righteous man named Simeon prophesies that Jesus would be a light even to the Gentiles. Twelve years later, the family comes to Jerusalem for the Passover. When they leave for home, Jesus stays behind and astonishes the teachers in the temple. His parents return for Him, but He explains He must be in His Father's house.

FOR MY BENEFIT

Jesus returns to Nazareth with his parents after the Jerusalem event. His parents did not understand what was coming, but His mother treasured all of this in her heart. She knew how special He was. This chapter is filled with prophecy and proclamations about the greatness of Jesus. We should treasure all of this in our hearts as well. The angels appear and praise God for the "peace on earth" that Jesus would bring. In the temple, Simeon holds Jesus in his arms and says to God, "My eyes have seen Your salvation." They believed He was God's gift to change the world. We know of His birth, His death, and His resurrection. We should openly proclaim His glory even more!

MY PRAYER

" *Heavenly Father, world history has two halves: before Jesus was born, and after. Thank You for blessing us to live in the days after Jesus came. So much anticipation and hope were tied to the coming of the Messiah. And by Your grace, He has come. May His worthiness dominate our hearts, and may He be "good news of great joy" every day of our lives. As a child, He wowed the teachers. His wisdom exceeds all men, including us. Help us to humbly be in awe of Him, to study His teachings, and to surrender our lives to follow Him.* "

THOUGHT QUESTIONS

God's only Son was birthed in a barn. What does that teach you about where and how God might begin wonderful things?

_____

_____

Simeon prophesied Jesus would be the Light for Jews and Gentiles. How has God had your salvation in mind since the beginning?

_____

_____

In His youth, Jesus prioritized the temple over traveling with His family. How does this foreshadow the message of the kingdom?

_____

_____

LUKE 3

John the Baptist's ministry begins as he preaches "a baptism of repentance for the forgiveness of sins." He fulfills Isaiah's prophecy as the one to come and to "make ready the way of the Lord." John speaks against many who come to be baptized, calling them "a brood of vipers" and instructing them to bear fruit in repentance. They want baptism, but they are not interested in fleeing from sin. John explains to them that true repentance means treating others fairly. Before John's arrest, he speaks of the mighty One who would come after Him bringing baptisms of the Holy Spirit and fire! He then baptizes Jesus, as the Spirit descends on Him and God speaks about Him from heaven! The chapter ends with the genealogy of Jesus back to Adam.

FOR MY BENEFIT

Three ideas from John's ministry set the tone for Jesus' teaching: baptism, repentance, and the forgiveness of sins. We must be baptized in water to have our sins washed away. Jesus' baptism sets an example for us. But we must also be willing to turn from sin, so that, by the planning and grace of God, our sins are forgiven. This choice is crucial as Jesus would bring two baptisms: the Holy Spirit in association with salvation or fire bringing destruction. The genealogy of Jesus is important because it proves Him to be the fulfillment of prophecies by connecting Him to both David and Abraham. He is God's choice from the beginning to be our Savior.

MY PRAYER

" Great God, You have the right to demand anything in order for us to become Your children. You have told us to believe in Jesus, to repent of our sins, and to be baptized in water. Thank You for showing this to us and teaching us how to receive the gift of the Holy Spirit. John was arrested for preaching these things. Help us to be bold in proclaiming this soul-saving truth to others. Jesus is the descendant of David, the seed of Abraham, Your plan for our salvation from the beginning. We praise His mighty name.

"

THOUGHT QUESTIONS

Many Jews desired baptism but were unwilling to repent. Are you willing to not only be baptized but continually turn from your sin?

_____

_____

When John teaches on repentance, he speaks of how we treat others. Is charity, fairness, and kindness to others important fruits of faithfulness?

_____

_____

Jesus was baptized, and then He began His ministry for God. How should we follow His example in baptism and in what comes after?

_____

_____

LUKE 4

The Holy Spirit leads Jesus into the wilderness. He fasts for forty days and faces intense temptation from the devil. Satan asks Jesus to turn rocks into bread, to accept kingdoms from the devil, and to jump and challenge God to catch Him. On each occasion, Jesus quotes scripture, gives credit to God, and refuses to fall in the face of temptation. Following this, Jesus comes to Nazareth, enters the synagogue, and asks to read from the book of Isaiah. He reads about the favorable year of the Lord and proclaims that the time has come! They doubt Him and even try to drive Him off a cliff! Jesus goes to Capernaum, where He is better received. He preaches the kingdom of God and casts out demons and heals many.

FOR MY BENEFIT

The devil uses three common tools to tempt Jesus: the lust of the flesh, the lust of the eyes, and the boastful pride of life. This is how he tempted Adam and Eve in the beginning, and this is how he tempts us. Jesus uses faith, Scripture, and wisdom to reject him, and we can do the same in His name. Jesus is the anointed One, and our Helper, and has ushered in a favorable age of victory over the devil. Jesus has proven His power in the wilderness, but also in casting out demons, healing the sick, and proving His limitless power. Even the demons proclaim Him to be the "Holy One of God." How much more so should we?

MY PRAYER

Gracious Lord, thank You for the example Your Son set for us in His ministry. Help us to be more like Him and see through the devil's common and carnal tools of temptation. To choose Satan is to reject Your Son, and we pray to flee evil and cling to Christ. Jesus brought us freedom from captivity and has shown us that He controls the spiritual and physical world. It is sad to see His hometown drive Him out. Please help us to always be humble and in awe of Him and to never push our King away.

THOUGHT QUESTIONS

Have you tried categorizing temptations? When you feel it coming, identify if Satan is tempting your eye, your flesh, or your pride.

_____

_____

Jesus' hometown could not accept that He was God's one and only plan to save them. Do you accept and embrace that fact today?

_____

_____

What does it say about Christ's glory that even the demons fear and confess Him as God? How must your faith be better than the demons?

_____

_____

LUKE 5

This chapter opens with three miracles of Jesus: filling the fishermen's nets with fish, healing a man filled with leprosy, and healing and forgiving the man who is lowered down through the roof. These works of God are among people of faith, as the result of faith, and lead to powerful results. The fishermen leave their nets and follow Jesus. The healed leper tells others about Jesus. The lame man goes away on foot, but most importantly he has his sins taken away. Amid this wonderful time, the Pharisees begin questioning Jesus. They accuse Him of blasphemy for forgiving sins. They question Him for eating with sinners at Matthew's house. They wonder why His disciples do not fast. Jesus explains that these are to be times of joy and feasting!

FOR MY BENEFIT

There is a great amount of faith and humility in these events. Peter says, "Go away from me Lord, for I am a sinful man!" The leper implores Jesus saying, "Lord, if You are willing, You can make me clean." And the lame man tasks several friends to tear a hole in the roof of a house to see Jesus. This contrasts strongly with the jealous, suspicious, self-centered Pharisees who looked for reasons to disbelieve. That group spent time fasting in sorrow when they should have been rejoicing in Jesus. Which of the contrasting groups best describes us? As disciples forgiven by Christ, we should be the most joyful, thankful, and evangelistic people on earth.

MY PRAYER

" *Dear Father, what a joy it must have been to sit and hear Jesus
preach, to watch Him fill nets and cure leprosy, and to see Him
forgive sins and sit with sinners to save their souls. Thank You for
preserving these stories in the Bible so we can learn of His mighty
works. We call upon Jesus' name for healing. But even more so, we
ask for Him to forgive our sins. Help us to be so grateful for that
gift that we tell others. And keep us rejoicing and feasting, even in
the face of trials.* "

THOUGHT QUESTIONS

There is action by the faithful in all our stories today. What action will
you take today because Jesus is the Healer and Forgiver?

Jesus touched a leper, and later He dined with sinners. What does this
teach you about how deeply Jesus cares for the hurting and the lost?

Jesus teaches it would be inappropriate to fast in sorrow while He is with
them. Is He with you? So, should we be fasting or feasting?

LUKE 6

The Pharisees continue their attacks on Jesus. They see His disciples picking grain heads on the sabbath and accuse them of breaking the law. Later, Jesus heals a lame man on the sabbath, and the Jewish leaders are enraged. In neither case has Jesus or His disciples done anything wrong. The hard hearts of the Pharisees are the problem. Following this, Jesus turns His attention to His ministry. He prays all night and then selects the twelve apostles. He works many miracles. He then gives the sermon on the mount. The focus here is on sacrifice in the kingdom, love for your enemies, and being fair in judging others. Jesus is addressing matters of the heart. To hear Him and obey Him is to build on an indestructible foundation.

FOR MY BENEFIT

The Pharisees turned their traditions into laws they bound on others. But Jesus alone creates laws for His people, and He is always right. We would do well to always acknowledge and understand those things. The greatest way to get out of a cycle of judgment is to get on mission. Jesus turned to recruiting workers, helping people, and preaching the gospel of the kingdom. These acts are great examples to help soften our hearts toward others. But we must practice what we preach: making sacrifices for the kingdom's sake, loving even our enemies, being merciful to others, and evaluating ourselves before critiquing others. These things come from the heart, and our hearts must be shaped by Jesus.

MY PRAYER

Tender Father, You have shown so much love in the life of Your Son. He led and fed His disciples. He healed the lame and forgave the penitent. He never let the religious leaders get in the way of His mission to seek and save the lost. It is a joy to serve a courageous and loving Savior. Help us to love Him, to hear Him, and to obey them. Give us opportunities today to be humble in spirit, to love our enemies, to be merciful to others, and to withhold unfair judgment. Establish us on the Rock.

THOUGHT QUESTIONS

It is tragic to think of what the Pharisees missed out on in Christ in the name of their pride. How can you make sure to never be like them?

_____

_____

Jesus' teaching is so counterculture: woe to the rich, love your enemies, give to others. Are you ready to be transformed for His name's sake?

_____

_____

The words you say come from your heart. This can be good or bad. How do you purify or soften your heart to help control your speech?

_____

_____

LUKE 7

A Gentile centurion sends for Jesus to come to heal a highly regarded slave. He notes that Jesus has the power to heal without being present. Jesus marvels at the Gentile's faith and heals his servant. Jesus later sees a funeral procession and feels compassion for a widow who lost her son. Jesus raises the young man from the dead and the people marvel! John the Baptist sends his followers to investigate these things. It was time for Jesus to increase while John decreased. Even so, Jesus speaks highly of John and his work. The chapter concludes with Jesus at a Pharisee's house. A woman comes and tearfully wipes Jesus' feet with her hair. Her humility outshines the Pharisee's pride, and Jesus forgives her sins because of her faith.

FOR MY BENEFIT

The characters in this chapter demonstrate the power of humility to access the blessings of Christ. The centurion sent for Jesus and considered himself unworthy for Jesus to come to his house. The Lord marveled at his faith and blessed him. John the Baptist is decreasing, even as he sends disciples toward Jesus. He knew his role and gave his life for the work. Meanwhile, the Jewish leaders keep accusing Jesus and judging others. Our identity comes down to two life pathways: the Pharisee, who invited Jesus in but showed Him no respect; or the sinful woman who cried for mercy at Jesus' feet. We can sit in pride and be lost, or we can bow in humility and receive mercy.

MY PRAYER

All powerful Father, we give all praise to You for Your glory and might. Lord God, help us to take all limitations off our belief. Like the centurion, help us to believe in the limitless scope of Christ's authority. When we hurt like the widow who lost her son, or the woman at Jesus' feet, lead us always to Him for help. We know we cannot be humble with others until we first are humble before our King. Father, challenge us directly to become more lowly before Him. Give us grace to live every day in peace with Jesus Christ.

THOUGHT QUESTIONS

Jesus marveled at the centurion's great faith. How can you have faith like this man in your life? Is it possible for Jesus to marvel at you?

The Pharisees deflected from their weaknesses by judging others. Do you ever do that? How do you prevent that behavior?

Jesus said those who are forgiven much, love much. Have you been forgiven much? According to Jesus, what should that mean?

LUKE 8

This is my favorite chapter in all the Gospels! Jesus tells His iconic parable of the Sower and the seed. The road, the rocky soil, the thorns, and the good soil represent four different states of the human heart. Only the fourth soil is fit for His kingdom, which represents a soft heart that is not distracted by temptation, worries, or wealth. What follows are four miracles that demonstrate the scope of Jesus' authority. He calms the sea, showing His power over the natural world. He drives out the demons, revealing He controls the spiritual world. He heals a woman who suffered for twelve years, showing He can heal the human body. And he raises a girl from the dead, exerting His control over the eternal spirit!

FOR MY BENEFIT

The main point of the parable of the Sower is to "take care how you listen." If we fail to listen, nothing changes. The message will get lost even as we listen if we also hear the noise of temptation, worry, or the love of money. Jesus is worthy to be heard and followed completely, above all else. And He has proven exactly why we should be fully committed to Him. He controls nature, and questions why disciples fear the wind and waves. He controls the spiritual world, and demons cower to His will. He can heal our bodies, and He will raise us from the dead and direct our souls to heaven if we live with full faith in Him.

MY PRAYER

Benevolent Father, thank you for the Sower and the seed. Thank You for sending Jesus and for the life-changing Gospel that has been shared with the world. We pray to hear Him and to let the Gospel saturate our hearts and be central to our lives. And we pray for the boldness to share it with others. He is glorious. He controls the physical world, the spiritual world, our bodies, and our souls. There is no escape from His rule and will. We pray that we never attempt to flee Him but live always at peace in His arms.

THOUGHT QUESTIONS

How do you regularly evaluate which type of heart you are developing? How do you strengthen your faith over fear, temptation, and worry?

_____

_____

Jesus expected His disciples to trust Him in the storm. This is easier said than done, but how do you do that when times are tough?

_____

_____

Jesus raised children from the dead in consecutive chapters. How does His power to resurrect impact the way you live each day?

_____

_____

LUKE 9

This chapter features interactions between Jesus and His disciples. He sends out the twelve to work miracles and proclaim the kingdom. He later challenges them to feed the multitude before doing so Himself. He asks them who they believe He is. They call Him "the Christ of God." They understand this, but they struggle to see that His mission demands His suffering and death. All who belong to Him must be willing to make sacrifices. Along the way, Jesus is transfigured on the mountain as His Father speaks from heaven! But His disciples still have much to learn. At times they lack faith to cast out demons and get distracted in arguments about who is the greatest. Jesus teaches them that full submission is required to be mighty in His kingdom.

FOR MY BENEFIT

Jesus' followers are a lot like us: they have their ups and downs. They can go from casting out demons to being unsure how to feed hungry people. They can be taught that the kingdom is a place of self-sacrifice, and then continue their argument about who is the greatest. Peter sees Jesus shine on the mountain, and he follows that with comments that suggest he understands very little. They can preach the gospel all over to save Jews, and then they ask Christ if they should destroy a village of Samaritans who disregarded Him. They are like us, and we can take comfort in that. Jesus was so patient with them, as He is with all of us.

MY PRAYER

Gracious Lord, we thank You today for the incredible patience Jesus has with His people. We, like the first-century followers, engage in the work, deny ourselves, and listen to Your Son with all our heart. And like them, we sometimes lack courage, get distracted by pride, and overreact to situations in a way that shows immaturity. He was so patient. And we praise You in gratitude that He continues to be patient. We know He will not tolerate excuses and split devotion. Please forgive our moments of weakness and help us firm up our resolve to serve Your beloved Son.

THOUGHT QUESTIONS

The 12 apostles worked miracles but later had issues with pride. What does that say about our need to grow, no matter who we are?

_____

_____

The Son of Man would have to die to save others. Is it unreasonable for Him to demand sacrifice on our part to carry out His work?

_____

_____

God said, "This is My Son, My Chosen One; listen to Him!" For you, today, how will you honor this command of the Father?

_____

_____

LUKE 10

Jesus selects seventy disciples and sends them out to work miracles and proclaim the kingdom of God. He instructs them to bless those who listen and move on from those who do not. Judgment is reserved for those who refuse to repent. As joyous as their works are, the greater blessing is having their names recorded in heaven. A lawyer then tests Jesus by asking Him what he must do to be saved. Jesus answers by quoting Moses concerning loving God and loving your neighbor. To illustrate, Jesus tells the story of the good Samaritan, who serves someone in need, even at a significant personal cost. The chapter concludes with Martha being busy and worried about so many things, while Mary chooses the better part: to sit and listen to Jesus.

FOR MY BENEFIT

Jesus often does His work through His people. We are His disciples, and sharing His love and power is our primary work. It can be discouraging when people do not listen. But that is not our focus. We, like the seventy, seek to teach all and pray the Gospel falls on soft hearts. Success in ministry is exciting, but our work is never as great as our names being recorded in heaven! Our primary objective is to love God fully and to always love our neighbor. Like the good Samaritan, we show Christ in how we love those who may not love us. To help develop this service, we need as much time at Jesus' feet as we can get.

MY PRAYER

Benevolent Father, thank You for initiating a kingdom and a mission that invites us to participate. We praise You for sending Jesus to show us the way. And we praise You for calling us to be like Him. Give us opportunities to share the Gospel. Keep us encouraged along the way. Help us deepen our love for you and others and demonstrate that in worshiping you and serving anyone in need. Father, like Martha, we can get distracted. While that may not be evil, it is dangerous. Show us how to fix our eyes on Jesus and listen to Him.

THOUGHT QUESTIONS

If Jesus called you with 69 others and sent you out to work on His behalf, would you go? How can you demonstrate that now?

_____

_____

Why is it so easy to pass people by who are in need? Is there a risk of becoming like the priest and the Levite who walked right by?

_____

_____

Martha was a faithful servant. But she lost sight of what mattered most. Do you ever get that way, and how do you regain your focus on Jesus?

_____

_____

LUKE 11

Jesus gives beautiful instructions on prayer. He teaches how to approach God, the importance of being persistent in prayer, and the crucial need for faith that God will answer. He proclaims that God sends His Spirit and that His answers are always good. Jesus follows this by casting a demon out of a mute man. At this point, the Pharisees come on the scene accusing Jesus of working with the devil! They ask Jesus for more signs to prove His relationship with God. Jesus strongly rebukes them and speaks of how Nineveh repented at the call of Jonah, and Israel does not repent at the call of God's Son! Following more accusations against Him, Jesus strongly condemns the Pharisees as hypocrites and as people guilty of leading others away from God.

FOR MY BENEFIT

Jesus demonstrates the most committed and accomplished prayer life of all time. When He speaks of how to address God, or how often to address God, or with what confidence we should address God, we would do well to listen. There will always be accusers like the Pharisees, and hypocrisy around us, but our connection with God is the power we must have to stand against them. This requires consistent, spiritual, and hopeful prayer. Sadly, unbelievers may never see enough to follow Jesus, and they may attack all they are shown. This manifests darkness, selfish pride, and brokenness in their hearts. Like Jesus, we must keep shining, patiently teaching, and warning others of the consequences of hardness toward God and others.

MY PRAYER

" Precious Lord, we are grateful to be able to come to You in prayer. Thank You for hearing us, for desiring this time with us, and for Your promise to respond according to Your divine will. We pray in Jesus' name. His authority and presence in prayer give us great courage. So many reject His Lordship. Some accuse Him, some question Him, while others will see His majesty and believe. Father, help us to always have believing, hopeful hearts. Please give us the wisdom to speak His name into the lives of those who are lost and confused.
"

THOUGHT QUESTIONS

How will Christ's teaching on prayer affect the way you talk to God today? Will You follow His direction, be frequent, and believe?

_____

_____

The Father gives the Holy Spirit to those who seek guidance (vs. 13). What does that mean to you, and how are you comforted by this?

_____

_____

Hypocrisy is ugly. Jesus always sees right through it. Is there some area of hypocrisy in your life where you need to be honest with Him?

_____

_____

LUKE 12

As the Pharisees become more aggressive, Jesus openly warns others about them. While some fear them, Jesus teaches that the only One worthy of fear is God, and they must show this by speaking up for Jesus in the face of opposition. Disciples must also defend the Holy Spirit's integrity against all who blaspheme. As Jesus is speaking, a man interrupts and asks for part of his family's inheritance. This displeases Jesus and leads Him to adjust His sermon topic. He addresses the sin of monetary greed. He speaks of putting trust in God and even selling possessions to help others. The most important thing is to be ready for Christ's return. These truths must be settled in their hearts because times of great persecution and temptation are coming.

FOR MY BENEFIT

Religious movements and groups can have a heavy hand of influence on believers. The only one we fear and answer to is God, and we must defend the Father, Son, and Spirit, no matter who speaks against them. This demands a sense of spiritual priority. It is so easy to get caught up in greed, too much focus on money, and a sense of dependency on things that are not of God. So many will not be ready when Jesus returns. We need to trust God, use our goods to help others, and always be ready to answer to our Lord. In the meantime, true faith can be divisive, and great trials may be in the near future. Get prepared today.

MY PRAYER

> *Powerful God, we fear You and offer worship and praise to You alone. Please help us to carry that same boldness into every conversation and every part of our lives. We get so distracted with worry and money and the judgment of others. Great God, help us to lean fully upon You, and to find rest in Your Son's kingdom. Please present us with opportunities to be givers and servants. All that matters is to be faithful to You at Your Son's return. Please help us keep that fresh in our minds as we face unbelievers and temptations in this life.*

THOUGHT QUESTIONS

The Pharisees were wrong, and their hypocrisy was dangerous. How does fearing God sometimes mean opposing religious people?

_____

_____

Greed is also very dangerous. How do you guard against it? What keeps you charitable and spiritual in this material world?

_____

_____

Are you ready for the Lord to return? How does the way you handle difficult people and temptation today help answer that question?

_____

_____

LUKE 13

Jesus uses two tragic stories of death to present His universal point: unless you repent of your sins, you too will likewise perish. Jesus tells a parable of a fig tree that would only remain if it began to bear fruit. Repentance is a turn from fruitlessness to bring about produce for the Lord. Shortly after, Jesus heals a woman, and the Pharisees complain because He did so on the Sabbath. They still are not ready to repent and turn to Him. But their attacks would not stop Christ's kingdom. It would start small and grow like a mustard seed or like leaven in flour. As Jesus heads to Jerusalem for the last time, He notes that few will be saved in His kingdom, though He desires to save everyone.

FOR MY BENEFIT

To repent is to be sorrowful for sin, to turn away from sin, and to run to God in trust and obedience. This is a fundamental attribute of kingdom citizens. God does not demand perfection, but His mercy is tied to our repentance. The kingdom, which started small, has grown all over the world as people turn from pride and self-reliance and to live for God. So many will be lost in the final judgment, living for themselves, and failing to prepare. But we must keep humble hearts until the end. Jesus faced death courageously because He believed in sharing the kingdom's message. We must praise Him for His sacrifice and share His message of repentance with all who will listen.

MY PRAYER

Loving Father, thank You for revealing Your plan to save us in the kingdom of Your beloved Son. Help us to see what is required of us in that plan: to believe and repent of our sins and live obedient lives. Give us the wisdom to do this faithfully. Show us how to live this faith sincerely, always ready for Your Son's return, and direct us to not be distracted with arguments and bitterness, as seen with the Pharisees. Eternal death awaits those who are unprepared. Keep us among Your people and help us reconcile others to You.

THOUGHT QUESTIONS

What does repentance look like in your life? Is it found in your prayers? Does it often produce change that is seen by others?

_____

_____

The kingdom grew as the Pharisee's influence diminished. Why is that? Why will genuine love and faith always prevail over hypocrisy?

_____

_____

Jesus wanted to save everyone but had to pronounce righteous judgment. Is there a time when we must do so with others for their good?

_____

_____

LUKE 14

Jesus dines with a leading Pharisee and sees a lame man there. Jesus heals him on the Sabbath, instructing the Pharisees to be humble and merciful. To help them, Jesus tells the story of a man who takes the best seat at a wedding feast and is asked to move down. Yet, the one at the foot of the table is moved up. Humility will be exalted. Jesus tells His host he should be inviting the poor and lame to his table. Such will be repaid in the resurrection. Jesus tells another story about people making excuses not to come to dinner, prompting the master to reject them. Christ's kingdom demands selflessness, service, love, and extreme cost. Jesus challenges them to calculate that cost, lest they fall short of His kingdom.

FOR MY BENEFIT

The Pharisees were watching Jesus closely in hopes of finding fault in Him. They failed to see His love and compassion for the hurting. They failed to see the value of taking the lower seat and serving others. Therefore, they did not invite the poor and lame to their tables. They, and others, made endless excuses and asked for endless signs instead of submitting to Jesus as their King. The Kingdom demands all of a person, their heart, mind, and soul. It means loving Christ and the ministry more than anything and anyone. We need to hear this clearly and calculate the cost. Many fall away because they were never totally committed. Discipleship to Christ is all or nothing.

MY PRAYER

Merciful God, please help us grow in compassion for others. Place people in our paths who are poor or lame or hurting. Lead us to develop selfless spirits that will be more like Jesus and help people who are in need. We will open our hearts, lives, and homes to be of service to others. Father, discipleship is a life-long challenge. Please forgive our failings and help us grow. May we never make excuses and always be willing to do better. Father, we have calculated the cost; we choose Jesus over all others, and we give our lives to You.

THOUGHT QUESTIONS

Has pride ever affected the way you see Jesus and His teachings? How do you reestablish humility and selfless love for others?

_____

_____

Why is it more Christ-like to invite the poor and hurting to your home over people with means or people who can also serve you?

_____

_____

What is the cost of discipleship in your life? What sacrifices are being made? Who must take a backseat so you can honor Jesus?

_____

_____

LUKE 15

Jesus is dining with tax collectors and sinners. The Pharisees and scribes grumble about this. They completely miss that Christ has come to seek and save the lost. To educate them on His mission, Jesus tells three parables. The first is a man who loses one of his one hundred sheep. He searches for the one, carries him back, and throws a party to celebrate. The second is a woman who loses one of her ten coins. She sweeps the house until she finds it, and then rejoices with her friends. The third is about a son who takes his inheritance and wastes it. He finally comes home, and the father throws a feast. His older brother is angry about this and must be taught about mercy by his father.

FOR MY BENEFIT

The point of all three parables is the same: our Father in heaven rejoices when even one soul repents of sin and returns to Him. We might not care about one sheep out of a hundred, but the Shepherd does. We might have lived with one lost coin, but the woman could not. We would certainly be crushed at losing a son, and we would throw a great feast if he returned home. This is why Jesus ate with sinners. He knew that every soul matters and the Father loves them all. The older brother in the Prodigal Son story struggles to have mercy on his brother. To be like our Father, we must be humble and welcome all who repent.

MY PRAYER

Patient Father, thank You for loving us and desiring our salvation. We know Your greatest joy is seeing a soul restored to Your care. Great God, if we need to repent and return to You, please show us the way. If we are lost sheep, please send Jesus to carry us back home. But Father, we also need to help others turn to You. Please cleanse our hearts of any pride that would look at others the way the older brother did, the way the Pharisees did. Send us someone today who we can lead back to You.

THOUGHT QUESTIONS

Jesus spending time with sinners was a shock to the Pharisees. Is it off-putting behavior to you? Should you be doing this also?

All three stories show how important repentance is to God. How should God's loving response to repentance affect all your decisions?

The older brother was self-centered and unmerciful. Does this ever happen today? Should Christians ever feel this way about others?

LUKE 16

Jesus shares a parable about a manager who squanders a rich man's possessions. Before being fired, he goes out and reduces debt for people who owe the rich man, in hopes that they will care for him after he is punished. The rich man praises the manager for his shrewdness! The point is we should use what we have now for righteous acts so we can be taken care of in heaven later. Otherwise, if we are unwise now, we will end up with nothing. This parable is told because the Pharisees love money. Jesus then shares the story of the rich man and Lazarus. Lazarus has nothing in this life but enjoys comfort in heaven. The rich man has much, shares little and ends up begging for mercy in torment.

FOR MY BENEFIT

The love of money is the root of all sorts of evil. Many are foolish and selfish with it and create many problems in their lives. We should think of money as a tool used to joyfully serve God and others now, ensuring a heavenly reward later. In the final parable, Lazarus rests in Abraham's bosom because, though physically poor, he was rich in faith. The rich man, in torment, would give every cent he had to be right with God, but he had nothing left to give. During his life, he knew God's law of mercy, but he was too busy enjoying his money. This story emphasizes a fundamental teaching of Jesus: we cannot serve God and wealth.

MY PRAYER

Benevolent God, to know You and be saved by You is the greatest treasure of our lives. All carnal things pale in comparison. Father, help this belief shape our daily lives and priorities. Show us how to be generous to others and use our blessings to be righteous and kind. We believe in eternal heaven and hell. But we sometimes forget that today's choices pave the way to our eternal home. Forgive our short-sightedness and open our eyes to Your Son's law of charity and mercy. Free us from the love of money and fill us with love for others.

THOUGHT QUESTIONS

How does your relationship with money change when it is seen as simply an asset to show faith to God and lay up eternal treasures?

There is a verse in this chapter on divorce and remarriage (18). How do greed and selfishness often factor into failed marriages?

Lazarus had nothing on earth, and he is now in eternal comfort. Can his story be a comfort to you or someone who is struggling in life?

LUKE 17

Jesus instructs His disciples: do not cause others to stumble, rebuke a brother in sin in order to help him, forgive those who repent, and keep laboring in this way throughout your life. Rest from these efforts comes in heaven. Jesus later heals ten lepers, but only one, a Samaritan, comes back to thank Him. Gratitude is a crucial element of faith and ongoing faithfulness. Pharisees then ask Jesus about the kingdom, and He explains that it is already in their midst. They are looking for a major political upheaval. One was coming, but not as they expected. It would be the destruction of Jerusalem as judgment for rejecting the Son of God. Jesus gives a deep description of what that will be like and how devastating it will be.

FOR MY BENEFIT

Jesus is protective of His brothers and sisters. We must see that and reflect that same love in the way we support our Christian family. There will be sin, and correction will be needed. But the goal is always repentance and fellowship. Sometimes this means our own repentance. This is not easy, but we are unworthy slaves of our King and must tirelessly pursue His ways. Gratitude will help. We, like the lepers, have been cured of a deadly disease. To come to Him and express thanks at His feet humbles us and helps us approach people with the right heart. Like the Jews did in 70 A.D., everyone will answer for their faith. Commit to deepening your trust in Him.

MY PRAYER

"Increase our faith!" We proclaim these same words the apostles uttered to Christ so many years ago. Deepen our trust, renovate our hearts, and make us more like Him in every part of our lives. We pray for more gratitude so that we can be much more open to extending grace to others. Your Son has healed us. He has saved us from the judgment to come. We acknowledge our responsibility in connection with that. We know this means being mindful of Jesus and doing everything we can to help reconcile others to You. Gracious Lord, please increase our faith!

THOUGHT QUESTIONS

How are you at forgiving others, or even the willingness to do so? Is this something worth praying about, and how will that help?

What has Christ done for you that makes you grateful today? How can that attitude fuel your thinking and words all day long?

Jerusalem was destroyed and only a few were prepared and survived. How do you stay ready and alert for the day of final judgment?

LUKE 18

Saving faith is defined by humility. Throughout this chapter, this is taught in many ways. It starts with persistent, thankful, modest prayer. How we approach God, and if we compare ourselves to others, says a great deal about us. This humility must persist after prayer and in how we treat those less fortunate than us. A ruler walks away from Christ because he will not sell his goods and help others. For those who are willing to do so, Jesus will care for them now and forever in heaven. Jesus demonstrates this entirely when He gives His life on the cross. So much of this for us is tied to our unworthiness. We are like the blind beggar, saved by the relentless pursuit of the love and mercy of Jesus Christ.

FOR MY BENEFIT

Jesus' teaching from Luke's perspective is quite challenging. It demands of us things we may easily understand, like prayer and trust and seeking Him diligently and fully. But then Jesus turns attention to how we see others. He demands we never elevate ourselves over others. He tells us to give up our own goods to help those who have less. Instead of telling us to be cautious about that, He demonstrates unprecedented charity by giving His life on the cross. He then challenges us to love like He loves. Would we have stopped to help the blind man? Part of growth is realizing that we are that man. But this must then extend to the compassionate way we see others.

MY PRAYER

" *Ever-present Lord, we thank You for always being willing to hear our prayers. We believe You always answer in a way that honors You and is good for us, according to Your will. Help us to self-evaluate as we pray. Teach us to be loving toward others, and to ask for wisdom to give, to serve, and to spread Your mercy and kindness to them. Your Son gave everything and now sits in glory. Show us how to pattern our daily lives after Him. Open our eyes to Him and give us the opportunity today to help others see His way.* "

THOUGHT QUESTIONS

How impactful is daily prayer in your life? If you are consistent and filled with thanksgiving, how will prayer be helpful to you?

Do you pray for others? Not just friends, but the needy, the hurting, and even those who don't love you. Why is this important?

"Son of David, have mercy on me!" Do you appeal to Jesus in this way? How does Jesus respond to genuine calls for healing and help?

LUKE 19

Compassion and repentance go together. Jesus has compassion for a tax collector by approaching Him, and Zaccheus responds by repenting of his sinful past. Jesus establishes a kingdom of workers who will carry His saving message. As the parable of the minas indicates, some will reject Him and be wasteful with their opportunities. But those who engage enthusiastically in sharing Him with others will be rewarded. As Jesus approaches Jerusalem for the last time, some worshipers gather to praise Him. But sadly, many in Jerusalem do not. It hurts Jesus to see so many reject His mercy. Jesus goes to the temple to drive out the greedy men and this enrages the Jewish leaders. These men prove to be the hateful and wasteful citizens from the parable of the minas.

FOR MY BENEFIT

Jesus went out of His way to help a tax collector in a tree, a man most would avoid. The parable of the minas, or even the talents, is only understood from this perspective. The work of cultivating His investment in us demands reaching people who are seeking Jesus. Evangelism is at the heart of discipleship. Jesus came to seek and save the lost. The Jewish leaders simply could not understand this. They wanted to protect their own established traditions, even though it had led to ungodly behavior, like money changing in the temple. They hated Him for demanding that they focus less on themselves and more on others. We must emulate Jesus and never these men of selfish motives.

MY PRAYER

Merciful Father, we are Zaccheus. We are sinners in search of someone to love us. Jesus has come, brought salvation to us, and challenged us to repent and lovingly serve Him faithfully. Lord, we are forever indebted to Him. Please give us the wisdom to know how to show that in the way we love, teach, and help others. You have invested in us, and we pray for the courage to multiply that investment. We will worship Your Son with boldness and joy. Please discipline us to focus less on self, money, and status, and more on kingdom ministry.

THOUGHT QUESTIONS

What would it require for you or me to derail our day to stop and notice Zaccheus and then go to his home? How can we be more like Jesus?

You belong to Jesus. This is such a peaceful place to be. How important is it for you to share that hope with people who need Him?

It seems money and greed kept the Pharisees too blind to see Jesus. What can you do each day to keep that from happening to you?

LUKE 20

It is easier to ask questions than to answer them, especially when one's motives are wrong. The Pharisees learn this lesson throughout this chapter. They ask about Christ's authority, but they cannot answer His question about the baptism of John. Jesus then tells a parable about workers in a man's vineyard. They beat his delegates, eventually kill his son, and they seek to take the vineyard for themselves. Judgment will be severe for such people. The Jewish leaders respond to this by asking Jesus questions about taxes and government, and then about marriage and the resurrection. On each occasion, He answers with integrity. He then asks them about David's son being Lord and they have no answer. Jesus warns people to beware of those who question but have no integrity.

FOR MY BENEFIT

There is no doubt that Jesus' teaching is powerful and demanding. Because of this, many in the world seek to diminish His authority and establish their own. A fundamental part of our faith is admitting that He has all authority to rule our lives. If He is relegated to a lesser role, our own desires will replace Him in the seat of our hearts. From there, many sinful things can happen. Jesus is faithful. He handles questions about Caesar, questions about the resurrection, and all questions with perfect wisdom. He knows infinitely more than we do. No question can stump the Maker of all things! If we doubt Him now, He will have difficult questions for us in the judgment.

MY PRAYER

Dear Lord, teach us how to have an all-in faith in Jesus. We have questions in this life. Help us to understand that our questions do not diminish His authority. Instead, they serve as more reason to trust in the One who knows all things. We have seen doubt turn to anger in the Pharisees and in people around us. How can we show them the peace that is found in surrender? Maybe that is seen in how we view the government. Or perhaps what we believe about resurrection. Give us opportunities to show the world we find our answers in Christ.

THOUGHT QUESTIONS

The Pharisees asked Jesus, "By what authority" He speaks and acts. How would you answer that question on your Savior's behalf?

_____

_____

Jesus was righteous when questioned about taxes and government. Why is it important to be peaceful and wise when asked about such things?

_____

_____

Questions about life after death can be very tough. Why is it important to defer to God and Scripture and trust that He will work it out?

_____

_____

LUKE 21

Jesus is at the temple and commends a poor widow for putting in all that she has to live on. This contrasts with those who give out of their surplus. Jesus has a message for those who deem the temple to be holy, but do not worship there with the right heart: the temple in Jerusalem will be destroyed. The disciples ask Jesus when such things will happen. Jesus tells them times will get tough and deceivers will abound. But it will be a great opportunity to testify to the truth. He instructs them to flee to the mountains when the judgment begins. Disciples will need to be on guard, stay prepared, and be willing to walk away when the time comes. This destruction would come in their generation.

FOR MY BENEFIT

The destruction of Jerusalem occurred in 70 A.D. Roman soldiers attacked the city, and many Jews were killed. Jesus warned about this, and those who believed in Him looked for signs, stayed ready, and escaped annihilation. There was much deception in those days. Disciples had to sift through error and be sure they were following the truth. The Roman army was the agency of Christ's judgment against the ungodly. We know that a final judgment is coming. Jesus will return personally, and He will destroy the world and those who are caught in deception. We can "stand before the Son of Man" if we listen, learn, and prepare for the coming of our King. The day of judgment is coming.

MY PRAYER

Powerful Creator, we live, move, and exist because of Your power and love. It brings great comfort to worship the One who created and controls all things. Father, give us the wisdom to see that this also means You have the power to destroy. As Jesus predicted Jerusalem's destruction, so will this world be burned with fire. Thank You for teaching us how to avoid judgment and stand with Jesus on the final day. We commit to being ready and embracing every opportunity to tell others to love and obey Your Son, and to prepare to meet Him face to face.

THOUGHT QUESTIONS

The temple was special to Jews, yet many had the wrong hearts. How important is your heart when you gather with others at places of worship?

_____

_____

Jerusalem's destruction was complete and terrible. How important is it to see that Jesus is willing to do this for those who reject His will?

_____

_____

Jesus warns you to be on guard, so your heart is not burdened by the worries of life. How do you work on that to prepare for His return?

_____

_____

LUKE 22

Jesus is the calm amid the storm as the end of His earthly life approaches. The Jews seek to kill Him. Judas has set up His betrayal. The disciples, while faithful, understand little and often devolve into arguments over who is the greatest. Peter makes a commitment he cannot keep. But in all this, Jesus remains faithful. He gathers the apostles and establishes the memorial supper that would have great meaning after His death and resurrection. He goes to the garden and communes with His Father. He is comforted by an angel and made ready to complete His mission. He quietly submits to arrest. While Peter's world is shattered by weakness in denying Jesus, the Savior tells the world He is God's Son, knowing it will lead to His death.

FOR MY BENEFIT

Satan is at work near the end of Jesus' life. He enters Judas to lead him to betray Jesus. He incites the jealousy of the Jewish leaders. He even demands permission to sift Peter like wheat and succeeds in tempting him to deny Jesus. Satan is a menace, then and now. He still features these same tactics: greed, fear, and pride. But Jesus is our anchor in the storm of Satan's efforts. Jesus gathers and protects His disciples. Jesus appeals to God on our behalf. Jesus communes with us in His memorial supper. And Jesus helps us face trials with composure and wisdom. We should always be anchored in Him and grateful for His help in times of need.

MY PRAYER

Holy God, we praise You during the trials and temptations of life. Satan tries to sow doubt and fear into our hearts. Father, give us clarity to see Your Son. He was focused, faithful, and always connected to You. His identity as Your Son sustained Him. Dear Lord, help us to be more like Him. Lead us to make more time for prayer and to keep our eyes on future hopes and blessings in Jesus. His behavior, even in the face of evil, was controlled by peace. Father, fill us with peace in knowing our triumphant King is always with us.

THOUGHT QUESTIONS

Why was Jesus so calm even as Satan was doing his work? How can you establish that kind of peace even if there is trouble around you?

Jesus' disciples struggled under trial because overconfidence led to complacency. How do you keep from complacency in your faith?

"Are you the Son of God?" "Yes, I am." Jesus confidently confessed His name. How does your faith in His identity help you daily?

LUKE 23

Pilate is a central figure in Luke's crucifixion account. He and Herod both question Jesus and find no guilt in Him. Pilate seeks to release Jesus, but the jealousy of the Jewish people is unrelenting. Pilate lacks the courage to save Jesus, but he demonstrates how an unbiased mind will see Him as holy. As Jesus is crucified, Luke's account notes three things Jesus says on the cross. He asks God to forgive His killers, for they do not know what they are doing. Jesus extends salvation to the repentant criminal. And Jesus commits His spirit into the Father's hands. These statements demonstrate His endless love and mercy and His complete trust in the Father. Following His death, a righteous man named Joseph is permitted by Pilate to bury Jesus.

FOR MY BENEFIT

Pilate is confronted with a choice: to side with an innocent man and risk his standing or to turn from Jesus and give in to the demands of sinners. We know he chose poorly. But if we see Jesus for who He is, then discipleship will be even more than just claiming His innocence. We must defend His honor. Perhaps Jesus' honor is best shown by who He was while dying on the cross. His words reveal the depth of His righteousness. We can see how deeply he loves mankind. In His image, we must prove our character by how we speak and behave under harsh and unkind treatment. Even in death, Jesus trusted that God would take care of Him.

MY PRAYER

Giving Father, You have shown Your grace in giving Your only Son to die on the cross to redeem us from our sins. We pray to have the cross always on our minds and to live each day in the shadow of that sacrifice. Help us to see His unrelenting love so that we will be drawn to Him, even after we have sinned against Him. We are the criminal on the cross, saved by Christ as we repent and turn to Him. Father, we also commit to a character that mirrors our Savior. Help us to shine in the darkness.

THOUGHT QUESTIONS

Pilate is such a tragic character. He knew the truth and lacked courage. What inspires you to stand for Jesus Christ against all opposition?

_____

_____

Both criminals mocked Jesus. One repented, and Jesus saved Him. What does that say about Jesus' willingness to save those who believe in Him?

_____

_____

A Centurion saw Jesus die and said, "Certainly this man was innocent." How important is grace under fire in showing righteousness to others?

_____

_____

LUKE 24

Women come to the tomb on the first day of the week and see two angels standing inside. The angels proclaim that Jesus is risen, just as He prophesied. Disciples then come to the tomb and marvel. That same day, Jesus appears to two men on the road to Emmaus, teaching them from the Old Testament scripture and revealing Himself to be the Christ. These men take this report to the eleven apostles in Jerusalem. Jesus then appears to the eleven and shows them the nail marks on His hands and feet, but they still struggle to believe. Jesus teaches them from the Scripture to firm up their faith and to prepare them for their ministry. He then ascends into heaven, as the disciples worship Him with great joy.

FOR MY BENEFIT

Luke's resurrection account openly notes how difficult it was for the disciples to believe. They did not initially believe the women's testimony about the angels. They did not believe the two men who reported their time with Jesus. They still could not believe, for a time, even after Jesus appeared to them! Throughout the chapter, Jesus uses Scripture to teach them about Himself and to help them believe their eyes. It can be difficult for people to accept the resurrected Christ. It is life-changing news. We must keep going to the Word to examine testimony and truth. Jesus was patient, and the disciples grew in maturity and service. Jesus is also patient with us, so we must be with others.

MY PRAYER

Great God, we believe! We believe Jesus died for us. We believe He was raised on the third day. And we believe that Jesus has ascended to rule in heaven. Great God, help us see how these truths should shape our daily lives and mission. The disciples worshiped Him with great joy and were continually praising You. Great Father, give us the humility to fill our days with praise. And please help our unbelief. Make Christ's resurrection the central part of who we are. Help us to be committed to being in the Word daily to learn more about our Savior.

THOUGHT QUESTIONS

Why did the disciples struggle to believe, even after all they had seen? They had much to learn to further fortify their faith. Do you?

Jesus went to the Scripture to prove Himself, though He could have worked any miracle. What does that say about the power of the Word?

Jesus died and was raised so a message of repentance and forgiveness could be preached to all. Who will you share that message with today?

JOHN 1

John's gospel starts "in the beginning." Jesus was the Word in heaven who made all things. After creation, He becomes the Light from heaven to illuminate our hearts. Jesus is the grace of God revealed to bring the Father's favor. He is the Lamb of God who would die to "take away the sins of the world." He is the Christ prophesied in the Old Testament. Jesus Christ is the greatest gift man has ever been given. John the Baptist proclaims Jesus as the Son of God, saying he has seen the Spirit fall on Him and that Jesus will be the One who baptizes others in the Holy Spirit. Jesus then begins his public ministry by calling into service four men from Galilee: Peter, Andrew, Philip, and Nathanael.

FOR MY BENEFIT

Most scholars contend that John's Letter is the last inspired Gospel. He brings a different perspective and unique details to Christ's ministry. The central point of his letter is belief. We must believe Jesus is the Creator. We must embrace Him as God's Light and grace, and as the sacrificial Lamb sent to save us from our sins. The evidence from John the Baptist, the Old Testament prophets, and the Holy Spirit falling on Him testify to Christ's identity. We must see Him as Nathanael did: with amazement and humility. Starting with simple trusting faith, Jesus takes Nathanael on an incredible journey and shows him many wonderful things. He will do likewise in our lives if we choose to follow Him.

MY PRAYER

Glorious Father, we praise Your Name for Your beautiful grace. Thank You for taking all the blessings You seek to give us and placing them in Your Son. If we will pursue Him, loving and obeying Him, we will be forgiven and saved forever. Great God, we ask you to take us on a journey like the four men who followed Jesus. Overwhelm us with Christ's glory. Then take us places we have never been, show us things we cannot imagine, and use us in ways we never thought possible. Lord, we believe. Show us how to follow Jesus.

THOUGHT QUESTIONS

Is Jesus your Creator? Is He God's greatest gift to bring grace and hope into your life? Why are those questions important?

_____

_____

John the Baptist was a great prophet, but he always redirected glory to Jesus. How do you direct all glory to Christ?

_____

_____

If Jesus showed up today and said, "Follow Me", would you go? How is He already calling you to do that in your life?

_____

_____

JOHN 2

The first recorded miracle of Jesus' ministry is the turning of water into wine in Cana of Galilee. His mother informs Him that the wine has run out at a wedding feast. While the time has not come for Jesus to show everyone His deity, He honors His mother's request, and He turns six waterpots into wine. This serves to "manifest His glory" to His disciples. Jesus then makes a trip to Jerusalem for the Passover feast. He makes a whip and drives out the money changers in the temple. The Jews ask for a sign as proof of His authority. He speaks of the temple being destroyed and rebuilt in three days. Jesus is referencing His death and resurrection. In Jerusalem, He performs signs, and many believe in Him.

FOR MY BENEFIT

The miracles in this chapter demonstrate the love of Jesus. He is easing into public ministry, but at His mother's request, Jesus turns the water into wine. This is a concession He makes out of love, and it encourages everyone. Later, in Jerusalem, while not yet time for Him to die, He still drives greedy Jews out of the temple. He does this because of His passion for bringing honor to His Father. Jesus is motivated by love, and He later dies on the cross to help others and obey God. We should appreciate how much He did out of concern for us, and we should emulate that by helping others and openly showing our love for our heavenly Father.

MY PRAYER

Worthy Lord, You deserve to be loved, worshiped, and obeyed. Your Son believed this so strongly that He drove out those who disrespected Your will. Lord, help us to be like Your Son, emotional about your worthiness and bold in the face of those who disobey You. Show us how to be motivated by love for You, but also our love for other people. Jesus often acted out of compassion and care, even altering His plans to be helpful. Lord, demand this of us. Create opportunities for us to serve others and demonstrate the heart of Christ in observable ways.

THOUGHT QUESTIONS

It was clear that Jesus loved His mother. Who in your life is so loved that you honor their requests even when it is not your desire?

_____

_____

The signs of Jesus "manifested His glory" and led to belief. In what ways do the miracles of Jesus lead you to stronger faith in Him?

_____

_____

Zeal for God led Jesus to aggressive behavior in the temple. Is there a time for that, and how must you be cautious in such moments?

_____

_____

JOHN 3

Nicodemus, a Jewish leader, comes to Jesus by night to proclaim his belief. Jesus states that a man must be born again of water and the Spirit to enter the kingdom of God. Nicodemus struggles to understand this concept. Jesus continues by announcing Himself to be the Son of God and stating that He is sent by God as the saving Light of the world and that He will "be lifted up" on the cross so that all who believe might be saved. John the Baptist spreads this message, baptizing those who come to him with open, repentant hearts. He states openly that Jesus is greater than him, the Son of God from heaven, and that all who believe in Jesus and obey Him will be saved for all eternity.

FOR MY BENEFIT

Salvation is only possible through Jesus Christ. He has come from heaven to show us the way. He was lifted up in death to become the payment for sin. Jesus is the Light of God, the hope of restoration in this world of darkness. We must believe in Him to be saved. This means "practicing the truth" and a willingness to "obey the Son." We must be born again in water to be renewed by the gift of the Holy Spirit. Jesus was baptizing people, as was John the Baptist. But baptism is only the beginning. Nicodemus struggled to understand and to change his life to follow Jesus. We must humbly decrease and let Christ increase and rule our lives.

MY PRAYER

Generous God, thank You for the Light from heaven that shines in the darkness. We believe that Your Son is our hope and Savior and that He sacrificed His own life to save us from our sins. Father, we may not always understand all that He teaches, but we pray to have hearts that always believe and humbly obey all that we know He is teaching us to do. Thank You for the gift of the Holy Spirit received at baptism. We will commit to obeying Your Son, the One who speaks Your Will and continually gives the Spirit without measure.

THOUGHT QUESTIONS

Nicodemus struggled to understand Jesus' teaching on being born again. What do you do when Christ's teachings challenge you?

_____

_____

How did God prove His love for the world? What should your daily and ongoing response be to this demonstration of love?

_____

_____

John the Baptist understands that he must decrease, and Jesus must increase. What does that process look like in your life?

_____

_____

JOHN 4

Jesus passes through Samaria on His way back to Galilee. He sees a Samaritan woman at a well and asks for a drink. She responds by questioning why a Jewish man would speak to her. What follows is a conversation wherein Jesus speaks of a gift from God, living water, that would spring up within her "to eternal life." The woman is both curious and cautious. Jesus patiently educates her about a relationship with God, independent of nationality. She knows a Messiah is coming, and Jesus openly tells her that He is the One. She believes and tells many others who then come to Jesus and believe in Him. Following this, Jesus returns to Galilee and heals a royal official's son by simply saying, "Go; your son lives."

FOR MY BENEFIT

Luke is the only Gentile author in the New Testament. His Gospel is committed to showing that Jesus' kingdom is open to all people. In this chapter, it is likely that the two beneficiaries of Christ's mercy are not Jews. The Samaritans were often maligned by the Jews, and yet Jesus preaches eternal life to a Samaritan woman. The official, whose son is sick, is often determined by commentators to be a Gentile. Salvation and the Lord's help are for those who believe in Jesus and worship God in spirit and truth. This means having hearts of faith and actions consistent with the teachings of the King. All who commit to these things have eternal life, regardless of nationality or background.

MY PRAYER

Father of Life, we know that living water and eternal life are found in You through Your Son Jesus Christ. Thank You for sending Him to find sinners like us. Thank You for sending a Savior who searches for a foreign woman with an immoral past. He is a Healer who changes lives in an instant wherever He encounters true faith. We are thankful for Jesus, and we trust in His power to help us. We will honor Him by worshiping You according to His teachings. Help us to worship with humble spirits, with absolute surrender, and with complete commitment to Jesus.

THOUGHT QUESTIONS

Jesus initiates a conversation with a woman in an uncomfortable setting. Why did He do that and how can you be more like Him?

True worshipers worship "in spirit and truth". How do you make sure to do this righteously when it comes to worshiping God?

The official believed Jesus and then his son was healed. Why is it crucial to believe the words of Jesus in order to be blessed by Him?

JOHN 5

Jesus returns to Jerusalem and heals a man who has been lame for 38 years. The Jews begin to persecute Jesus for healing on the Sabbath day. Jesus responds by proclaiming that He is carrying out His Father's work. The leaders understand Jesus to be claiming a special relationship with God, so they seek to kill Him. Jesus claims to be sent by God and presents testimony to prove it. Firstly, the preaching of John the Baptist verifies the deity of Jesus. Secondly, the miracles of Jesus prove His heavenly power. Thirdly, the Old Testament Scripture, including the teachings of Moses, prophesy concerning Jesus as the Messiah. Jesus has the authority to speak for God and He will be the final judge over all men on the last day!

FOR MY BENEFIT

It must have been incredible to be healed by Jesus after 38 years of illness. Jesus levels a powerful message to the healed man: "Do not sin anymore, so that nothing worse happens to you." Surely this man lived the rest of his days in faithfulness to God. The Jewish leaders were too busy arguing about Sabbath rules to see the amazing things Christ was doing. We must be like the healed man and not the Pharisees. We are healed from a life of sin by Jesus. And we are charged with faithfulness in His honor. Jesus has proven His power to save and direct us. If we stay humble, we will have compassion for everyone who needs Jesus.

MY PRAYER

Dear Father, before Jesus found us, we were burdened by sin and unable to stand justified on our own. But Your Son has saved us by His grace. Help us to live every day in thankfulness to Him. He has also directed us to flee from sin and honor His Lordship. Please teach us how to do those things joyfully. Strengthen us to have hearts of faith that believe the testimony about Jesus, and hearts that lovingly adore Him and care about others as much as He does. We will love Him and live in readiness for His return.

THOUGHT QUESTIONS

What has Jesus healed in you that was previously a heavy burden? Are you thankful enough to "not sin anymore" in His honor?

_____

_____

Jesus provided testimony to prove His Lordship. What evidence would you provide to convince someone Jesus is God?

_____

_____

Jesus is coming again in the final judgment. Are you ready for that day to come? How do you do your best to stay ready?

_____

_____

JOHN 6

Jesus feeds 5,000 people with five loaves and two fish. The people proclaim Him as the Prophet of God. They want to make Him king, so He withdraws to the mountains. His disciples then cross the sea to Capernaum. Several miles out, in high winds, Jesus walks to them on the water! He gets in the boat, and they are immediately at the land. The crowd from the previous day crosses the sea looking for Him. Jesus explains they come to be fed, but that He is the bread of life. All who digest His words will be raised on the last day and live forever! Sadly, many are confused and leave Him. But the twelve apostles remain saying, "Lord, to whom shall we go? You have the words of eternal life."

FOR MY BENEFIT

Jesus performs physical signs to validate spiritual messages. When He feeds the people, some think of Him as a source of physical blessings. But the miracle is simply to demonstrate that He is the Source and Sustainer of life. His nourishment is truth, love, and forgiveness. He fills us with His goodness and spiritual promises so our souls will never lack and will live forever! God gave Israel manna, but they died in the wilderness. God has given us Jesus so that we may live now, and forever after the final resurrection. Jesus' teaching is not always easy to understand or follow, but to whom shall we go? He is the Holy One and He has the words of eternal life.

MY PRAYER

Holy God, Your Son is a miracle worker. He feeds thousands. He walks on water. He calms the storm. It is not just what He does that draws us, but who He is. He is Your Son. He is the bread of spiritual and eternal life. He is the Prophet who promises a future resurrection into the glory of heaven. He is everything to us. Lord, fill our hearts with thanksgiving and embolden our lives and lips to pronounce His majesty. When we struggle to under-stand, hold us close and help us learn to trust Him in all things.

THOUGHT QUESTIONS

Christians understand that following Jesus is about spiritual richness over physical provisions. How do you show that in your life?

_____

_____

Jesus says to eat His body and drink His blood. In practical Christian terms, what does that look like in your walk of faith?

_____

_____

When things got hard, many disciples left. What keeps you serving Jesus when His will is difficult to understand or follow?

_____

_____

JOHN 7

Jesus' unbelieving brothers encourage Him to go to Jerusalem and publicly work miracles. Jesus refuses and later goes up more privately, and He eventually enters the temple and teaches the people. He gives all glory to His Father for His words of wisdom. Though many believed in Jesus when He acknowledged having come from the Father, many Jewish leaders sought to kill Him. Jesus makes a series of beautiful claims. He is soon to return to His Father. All who come to Him with spiritual thirst will be gifted a flowing river of living water. Those who believe in Him will be given the Holy Spirit. These messages divide the crowd. Some proclaim Him as the Christ, but the Pharisees will not believe and become even more angry.

FOR MY BENEFIT

Even Jesus' brothers had doubts about Him before His resurrection from the dead. Jesus continues to be patient with them and with all His disciples in His teaching. He is also insistent that He has come from the Father, and He has all authority to teach and would be returning to the Father. The kingdom would leave no middle ground for disciples to believe in His blessings without also trusting in His Lordship. Jesus will come and take us home with Him. He will fill us with eternal life and the Holy Spirit. But there cannot be doubt within us. We must confidently assert Him to be "the Prophet" and "the Christ", even in the face of those who reject Him.

MY PRAYER

God of Grace, You have shown Your deep love for us in sending Jesus to guide us back to You. Thank You for His ministry, His wisdom, and the undeniable proofs of His Sonship. So many will not believe in Him. So many are inconsistent in their willingness to obey Him. We pray for the resolve to put our lives in the hands of the Prophet and to surrender to Him as the Christ. Please fill us with salvation from Your Holy Spirit. We also ask for boldness to always defend Your honor and to invite others to surrender to Jesus.

THOUGHT QUESTIONS

Many hated Jesus because He exposed their sinful deeds to be evil. Do you also have to see sin as evil to be a follower of Jesus?

Jesus always redirected glory away from Himself and to the Father. In what ways should we be openly redirecting all praise to God?

The Pharisees rejected all testimony about Jesus. What leads hearts to be that hard to truth, and how do you avoid that same fate?

JOHN 8

Jesus is teaching in the temple when Jewish leaders bring Him a woman who has been caught in adultery. They ask Him what should be done to her. He asks the one who has no sin to cast the first stone. Slowly, all the men leave. He then explains there is no testimony against her and sends her away, telling her to "sin no more." This opens a discussion about testimony concerning Jesus, including His own words and works, along with the prophecy and proclamations of His Father. He teaches eternal life with the Father and that unbelievers will die in their sins for the devil is their father! The men try to claim Abraham as their father, but Jesus enrages them when He says, "Before Abraham was, I am".

FOR MY BENEFIT

Things are heating up between Jesus and the Jewish leaders. He is teaching in their temple and embarrassing them with His wisdom. In the case of the adulterous women, the men's motives are faulty, and they leave in shame. But the guilty woman is given a pardon by the mercy of the Lord. Jesus has proven His glory and His right to be obeyed, and those who will not believe will die in their sins. To claim God as Father is to follow Jesus. We must understand this. To follow the world is to have the devil as our father. We belong to whomever we follow. Jesus existed before all men, is glorified as holy, and is worthy to be praised.

MY PRAYER

Kind Father, we know You show mercy to those who are sorrowful for their sins. Like the adulterous woman told to sin no more, we call upon your grace to free us from our sins, and we vow to pursue holiness. We acknowledge Your Son as the Light of the world, and the One who was lifted up to save us from sin and darkness. He is eternal and He is holy, and reverence to You is shown through belief in Jesus and obeying His teachings. We commit to Him as our Guide and to You as our only Father.

THOUGHT QUESTIONS

Beyond the fact that all witnesses left, why did Jesus send the adulterous woman away unpunished? What does that say about Him?

_____

_____

Jesus said you must continue in His word to be set free from sin. How are you making it a priority to continue in His word?

_____

_____

Can God be your Father if He is not allowed to control your life? Why must you trust and follow Jesus to have God as your Father?

_____

_____

JOHN 9

Jesus heals a man who is blind from birth. As the Light of the world, Jesus puts clay on the man's eyes and renews his sight. The Pharisees question the man as to what has happened, and the man announces Jesus as a prophet. The Jews then call in the man's parents, confirming he was born blind. They will not believe in Jesus and are determined to discredit the miracle. They speak to the man again, and he proclaims the Healer to be from God. The Jewish leaders then put him out of the synagogue. Jesus finds the man and reveals Himself to be the Son of Man, and the healed man worships Him. Jesus then teaches that Pharisees who think they can see will always be blind and in sin.

FOR MY BENEFIT

The blind man's healing leads to these words of Jesus: "For judgment I came into the world, so that those who do not see may see, and that those who see may become blind." For all who are humble and in need of Christ, He brings light and restoration. The blind man represents all sinners, in need of opened eyes by the power of Jesus. If He has restored us, we should openly and passionately worship Him as the Son of God. But those who think they see without Him will not come to Him for healing. All who choose to reject the glory of Jesus will be revealed in the end as blind and lost in darkness.

MY PRAYER

" Dear Lord, You have shown amazing mercy in sending Your Son, the perfect Light, into this world of darkness and sin. He relentlessly seeks those who know that they need Him. Father, we pray for an ever-present need for the Light of the world in our lives. We are often blind and drawn to the shadows. Will You please make Jesus the Light to our path and the One who shows us the way? Give us the wisdom to see Him and follow Him. Purge from our hearts any arrogance, pride, and disbelief that would keep us from our Savior. "

THOUGHT QUESTIONS

The man's blindness created a circumstance for God to act. Are you open to seeing your struggles as opportunities for Christ to work?

_____

_____

The healed man worshiped Jesus. Do you believe Jesus is worthy of your worship? How does that look on days other than Sunday?

_____

_____

The Pharisees would not believe no matter the evidence. What creates that sort of blindness and how do you avoid it?

_____

_____

JOHN 10

Jesus likens His disciples to sheep who hear His voice and follow Him. Jesus is the gate that they enter to reach safety. He is also the good shepherd who calls them forth and leads them in green pastures. He alone has authority over them. A good shepherd will put his life on the line for the sheep. Jesus proved this by dying on the cross for the good of His people. He would also be raised from the dead and continue as their shepherd in heaven! The Pharisees reject all of this, and once again revile and accuse Him. He tells them they say these things because they are not of His sheep. His works prove He is the Son of God and that all should believe in Him.

FOR MY BENEFIT

The sheep and shepherd imagery are valuable for believers. Jesus is not just our Savior; He is our Shepherd. We do not simply believe in Him, we follow Him. Jesus has authority over our lives. We answer His call. We go where He directs us. Jesus has earned this right by laying down His life to save us from the enemy. He has also risen and is ruling at the right hand of the Father. The Pharisees rejected Jesus' message because it would mean surrendering their power to Him. They could not see past their desires. True belief involves total surrender. The choice is ours, but the testimony about Him will condemn us if we do not believe in Him.

MY PRAYER

Great God, please allow us to honor our Savior with this adaptation from Psalm 23: The Lord is our shepherd. We shall not want. He makes us lie down in green pastures; He leads us beside quiet waters. He restores our souls; He guides us in the paths of righteousness for His name's sake. Even though we walk through the valley of the shadow of death, we fear no evil, for He is with us. Surely goodness and lovingkindness will follow us all the days of our lives, and we will dwell in the house of the Lord forever.

THOUGHT QUESTIONS

What does it mean in your daily life for Jesus to be your shepherd? How do you go about living as a sheep within His flock?

_____

_____

How has Jesus demonstrated a depth of love for you that goes beyond what anyone could ever do? How do you honor Him?

_____

_____

Evidence for Jesus as God's Son is powerful and life changing. What testimonies about Christ have the deepest impact on you?

_____

_____

JOHN 11

Lazarus is a friend of Jesus and the brother of Mary and Martha. Jesus hears that Lazarus is sick and informs His disciples that this illness will bring glory to God. Jesus delays His trip to Bethany, knowing that Lazarus will die and then be raised from the dead. As He approaches the village, Jesus tells Martha her brother will rise again. Jesus follows this by announcing Himself as "the resurrection and the life." He then calls for Mary and weeps as he sees her despair over her brother's death. Jesus then raises Lazarus from the tomb. This results in more people believing in Him. The Jewish leaders, however, are confounded on how to handle Jesus. By the prophecy of high priest Caiaphas, they plan to put Him to death.

FOR MY BENEFIT

John's Gospel includes seven miracles from Jesus' ministry. No miracle of Jesus is greater than raising Lazarus from the dead. This proves His power over life and death. His death and resurrection would also confirm this power. We can live by faith, without fear of death, knowing that Christ will revive us again and give us eternal life. Even though death has no power over Him, Jesus still weeps at the sorrow of people who mourn their loss. Our Savior's miraculous might does not diminish His compassion for His people. Sadly, the Jewish leaders would not believe in the saving power of Jesus, as they wanted lives free of His influence. We must never give in to such a devastating decision.

MY PRAYER

Benevolent Father, You always provide what we need and bless us with Your mercy. We trust You in life, but Father, we pray to also do so in the face of death. We thank You for the ministry of Jesus and the scope of His power. Of all that He has done, we treasure most His victory over death. Since He raised Lazarus from the grave, we know that death is not the end for us. Help us to take comfort in this during our lives, but also that we keep the faith through to the end, knowing eternity is coming.

THOUGHT QUESTIONS

Jesus loved Lazarus and his family. And yet, Jesus allowed him to die. Why? And how can that bring comfort to us in times of loss?

Do you have faith that a believer "will live even if he dies"? How does eternal life in Christ shape the way you make daily decisions?

Jewish leaders wanted to kill Jesus because they feared Rome's involvement. How is faith impossible if you fear worldly forces?

JOHN 12

Jesus and His disciples come to Bethany to dine with Mary, Martha, and Lazarus. Mary anoints His feet with costly perfume. Judas Iscariot grumbles about this because he is a thief and hopes to plunder money from the sale of the perfume. A large crowd gathers to see Jesus and the resurrected Lazarus. This infuriates the Jewish leaders, who plan to kill Lazarus. Jesus then enters Jerusalem, and His followers worship Him as King. Many come to Jesus, including Greeks who had come to Jerusalem for the Passover feast. Jesus teaches them that personal sacrifice is needed to be in His kingdom. The people then hear God, from heaven, proclaim Jesus and His glory! Some follow Him, while others who believe are silenced by their fear of the Jews.

FOR MY BENEFIT

The approval of men, and fear of others, are serious tests of faith. To believe in Jesus is to follow His teachings, leaving darkness for light, no matter what anyone thinks. The world, in so many ways, tries to weaken and silence believers. Judas was weakened by greed, and he betrayed the Lord. The Pharisees were blinded by jealousy and selfishness. Though God from heaven pronounced Jesus as worthy, others feared the actions of men and would not confess Jesus as King. In all of this, there are servants like Mary, who poured her expensive oil on Jesus' feet with no concern for what anyone thought about it. Only those who believe like Mary will be saved on the last day.

MY PRAYER

> *Holy God, we love You and desire to grow in our service to You and Your Son. Help us to see how that must resemble Mary pouring oil on Jesus' feet. Lead us to see ourselves bowed down to worship Jesus as He rides in on a colt. This world and its darkness seek to overwhelm us and make us ashamed of Jesus. Give us the strength to fight against greed and jealousy. Help us develop the courage to live out a sacrificial faith in Christ, regardless of what anyone says or does. We know "that His commandment is eternal life."*

THOUGHT QUESTIONS

We cannot replicate Mary pouring expensive oil on Jesus' feet. But what does it look like for you to be more like her?

_____

_____

Jewish leaders rejected Jesus, while Greeks sought to speak with Him. What does that say about where faith might be found?

_____

_____

Jesus had to "be lifted up" in death to save us from our sins. Are you also willing to face mistreatment in order to carry out the mission of God?

_____

_____

JOHN 13

Jesus gathers with His twelve apostles for a Passover meal just hours before He is arrested. He begins by washing the feet of each of the men. Peter is reluctant to allow this, but Jesus insists. Jesus teaches them that the service of others is at the center of His kingdom. Jesus then tells them that one of His own will betray Him. No one knows that He is referring to Judas Iscariot. Satan fills Judas' heart, and he flees. Jesus then explains that His time of departure and glorification has come. He tells them the most important thing they can do is to love each other. Peter insists on going with Jesus, but he is told that He is not ready and that he will deny Jesus that very night.

FOR MY BENEFIT

This is the night in which Jesus would be betrayed and arrested, and yet His focus is on teaching His disciples to care for one another. By washing their feet and later teaching them about the crucial need for love, He is demonstrating what makes His kingdom strong in the face of any trial. In our shared walk, there will be betrayers who give in to this world. There will be ignorance, like the apostles who had no idea who would betray Jesus. There will be disappointment, like Peter's predicted denial of Jesus. God's people can remain united and strong if we sacrificially serve, deeply love, and tirelessly support one another. That is the kingdom of believers Jesus died to establish.

MY PRAYER

Great Father, we praise Your glorified Son, and we lament that He was subjected to betrayal, suffering, and death on our behalf. We know He now rules in glory because of His incredible sacrifice. It endears us to Him to see Him washing feet and teaching love in the moments before His arrest. Help us to have a spirit like His. Teach us how to serve one another so that the world may know us by our love. Like Peter, we often fall short due to a lack of understanding and pride. Forgive us and help us to grow together.

THOUGHT QUESTIONS

Jesus said disciples "ought to wash one another's feet." What should that look like in your life and relationship with Christians?

_____

_____

Judas was so crafty that no one, except Jesus, knew of his sins. If only Jesus knows of your sins, is that enough reason to repent?

_____

_____

Peter wanted to die with Jesus, but he was not yet ready. How are you developing the kind of faith that would give your life for Jesus?

_____

_____

JOHN 14

J esus says twice to His apostles: "Do not let your heart be troubled." Jesus first tells them not to worry because He will go to heaven to prepare a place for them, and then He will return to take them home. They did not understand where Jesus was going, but He goes to the Father and is in perfect unity with the Father. Jesus explains that His disciples must honor Him by keeping His commandments. All who love Jesus must obey Him. Jesus assures the apostles He will send a Helper, the Holy Spirit, to teach them how to establish His church. A second time, He tells them not to be troubled because the Spirit's presence will help them live with peace so that they can accomplish His work without fear.

FOR MY BENEFIT

This chapter takes place during the Passover meal Jesus engages in with His apostles. Some of what is included is specific to those men, like the promise of the Holy Spirit to give them special knowledge. However, much of His teachings apply to all believers. Jesus has gone to heaven, and He will return to take home all who love Him and obey His commandments. In the meantime, we can live in peace because God loves us, and the Holy Spirit is active in helping us develop fearlessness in this life. The "ruler of the world" is among us and seeks to undermine our faith. But we believe that Jesus is with the Father and rules in victory over the adversary.

MY PRAYER

" *Wonderful Father, we call upon You to help us develop peace deep within our hearts. "Do not let your heart be troubled." We hear the words of Jesus and seek to live this joy and assurance deep within us. Will you please help us to find this strength? We know the strength is in the resurrected and ruling Christ. And we know the Holy Spirit's help is readily available in the Scripture. Please help us to remember to fill our lives with prayer and Bible study. We love and obey You, and we know that You love and protect us.* "

THOUGHT QUESTIONS

What causes your heart to be troubled? And what do you know about the Father, Son, and Spirit that restores your peace?

_____

_____

Jesus is the only way to be close to the Father. How are you pursuing a closer relationship with the Father through Jesus?

_____

_____

The Holy Spirit helped the apostles in incredible ways. How does the Holy Spirit help you in your walk and work for Christ?

_____

_____

JOHN 15

Jesus continues His discourse with the apostles. Jesus identifies Himself as "the true vine." His followers are like branches that draw nutrients from Him. To "abide in Him" is to be connected to Jesus, to hear His words, and to gain strength from His power. This must result in good fruit born by the branches. To bear the fruit of good works is to prove to be His disciple. Love binds the Vine to the branches. Jesus has shown His love by laying down His life for His friends. His friends show love in return by keeping His commandments and loving one another. The world hates Jesus and His followers, but love will define His people. Jesus again promises the apostles that the Holy Spirit will help them in their work.

FOR MY BENEFIT

As noted in the previous chapter, some of this content is unique to the apostles. The Holy Spirit would testify through them in miraculous ways. The Holy Spirit is also at work for us; He teaches us through the Scripture. Many other elements of this chapter apply to us all. Jesus is the vine, and we are the branches. We must remain connected to Him and bear fruit, lest we be cut away by the Father. Specifically, Jesus demands that we keep His commandments and love our fellow believers. We will be maligned by the world for serving Jesus because people of the world reject His Lordship. But fellow Christians should always be a source of love and support.

MY PRAYER

" Creator God, we know that You have made us to bring honor to You. And that means living obedient lives and loving others the way You love us. Will You help us see how desperately we need Jesus to do these things? Show us how to connect to Jesus and how to draw our strength and direction from Him. We are committed to bearing the good fruit of obedience and love in a world of disobedience and hate. Show us how to love Christians in an enduring way, and please help us through the presence and teachings of Your Holy Spirit. "

THOUGHT QUESTIONS

Are you abiding in Christ and bearing fruit through His strength? What are observable ways you demonstrate this process to others?

_____

_____

The Lord has commanded us to love one another. Can your faith be a saving faith if you do not actively love and serve Christians?

_____

_____

The worldly have no excuse for living in sin and disregarding the King. How can you help them see their need for Jesus?

_____

_____

JOHN 16

Jesus continues to prepare His apostles for the difficult times that are approaching. After Jesus ascends, religious people will seek to kill these men, falsely believing that such attacks honor God! Fortunately, the Holy Spirit is coming to guide the apostles into all truth and disclose what is coming. Jesus must ascend into heaven so that He can send the Holy Spirit to them. But that process will be painful; Jesus will first have to be arrested, beaten, and killed. While this will be a time of great sadness, Jesus assures them He will rise again and appear to them. The disciples will be scattered when Jesus is arrested, but He will rally them to Him after He is raised. Peace will prevail because Jesus will overcome the world!

FOR MY BENEFIT

The days of Christ's arrest and death are the darkest in human history. But they were necessary to bring about God's plan for our redemption. Jesus' victory over death overcomes the world in that sin and death no longer have power of His followers. His death also brought about the new covenant that God intended from the beginning of time. The Holy Spirit has come to earth as the result of Jesus ascending to glory. Jesus has sent Him to teach us concerning sin, righteousness, and the judgment to come. We are immensely blessed by Jesus' death, burial, resurrection, and ascension into heaven. Though times of sadness and tribulation may come, we live with abiding peace in the victory of Jesus.

MY PRAYER

Kind Father, we praise You and thank You for the revelation of Scripture. You have disclosed to us the life and victory of Jesus, as well as the teachings of the Holy Spirit. You have warned us of the world's response to truth, preparing us to stand firm in faith and to avoid stumbling in confusion and doubt. Father, help us develop the discipline to study the words of Jesus and to read the Spirit's revelation concerning sin, righteousness, and the judgment to come. Teach us how to live by faith in Christ, the One who has overcome the world.

THOUGHT QUESTIONS

What has Jesus revealed in the Gospels that keeps you from stumbling? What gives you the courage to be strong in faith?

_____

_____

What has the Spirit taught you in Scripture about sin? What has He shown you about righteousness? What about the judgment to come?

_____

_____

A woman birthing a child goes from pain and weeping to great joy. How does the resurrection of Jesus move you from sorrow to joy?

_____

_____

JOHN 17

This is one of the most beautiful chapters in all of Scripture. It documents a prayer offered by Jesus while He is with His apostles. Jesus speaks of all things leading back to the Father. Whatever glory and authority Jesus has, He uses it to turn all attention to the Father and His gift of eternal life. He committed his life to accomplishing the will of the Father. Jesus is soon to depart, and He prays that God will keep the disciples in the faith and unified with one another. Jesus asks for God to keep them from the evil one and to sanctify them in the truth. He then prays for all believers that they may be one, perfected in unity, striving together in the love of God.

FOR MY BENEFIT

The most striking aspect of this prayer is the incredible humility of Jesus. He defers all glory to His Father, addressing Him as holy and righteous. All that Jesus has been gifted to do is used to turn the world toward the Father. This is a lesson that should live on in us. We are agents for God, and all the glory and authority we have is to direct people back to Him. Jesus then prays fervently concerning His disciples. He prays for their unity, and their strength, and that they live in sanctity and love. If we are genuinely interested in honoring the Father in this life, we must invest fully in the strength and unity of fellow believers.

MY PRAYER

" *Holy and righteous Father, You are worthy of all praise and glory. Even Jesus, the Savior of the world, gives honor to You. Great God, demand of us the service and loyalty that You deserve. In You is eternal life, and we devote our lives to service and gratitude for this incredible gift. Father, Your Son has taught us to love one another. Unity among Christians was the Savior's prayer, and we make it ours as well. Please help us overcome the issues and attitudes that divide us. Sanctify us together in truth and keep us from the evil one.* "

THOUGHT QUESTIONS

Jesus knew His death was coming, and He welcomed it to honor God. How will you be like Him when difficult times come?

_____

_____

Jesus prayed that God would protect His friends from Satan. Who will you ask God to protect from the enemy today?

_____

_____

Why do you think there is so much division among God's people? How can Jesus' prayer for unity help us all?

_____

_____

JOHN 18

Jesus takes His apostles into a garden, where Judas and Roman officers come to arrest Him. Peter cuts off a soldier's ear, but Jesus replaces it and goes with the soldiers peacefully. Peter and John follow closely behind as Jesus is taken before Annas, and then Caiaphas, the high priest that year. Peter is then questioned concerning Jesus, and he denies Him three times. The Jewish priests lead Jesus to Pilate since they need Roman approval to put Him to death. Pilate asks Him if He is the King of the Jews. Jesus responds by stating that His kingdom is not of this world. Ultimately, Pilate sees no guilt in Jesus. He asks the Jews if he should release Him, but they demand that a convicted robber be released instead.

FOR MY BENEFIT

There is an incredible calmness in Jesus as the time of His death approaches. When Peter injures a soldier, Jesus heals the man. When soldiers seek to arrest Him, Jesus simply asks that His followers be left alone. When questioned by the Jewish leaders, He answers by stating that He has kept no secrets in His ministry. As Pilate berates Him with questions, He answers with peaceable, spiritual, truthful answers. Meanwhile, Peter denies Him, and most of the apostles are nowhere to be found. Our Savior is at peace with His purpose and with the sacrifice He would offer for the world. Peter and the apostles became much more like Jesus after the resurrection. This should be our goal as well.

MY PRAYER

Gracious Lord, thank You for Jesus. His confidence and calmness establish Him as a King we are privileged to follow. Even in the fires of persecution, He was focused and holy. He answered even His most vicious accusers with dignity. Lord, teach us how to be more like Your Son. We all falter at times, resembling Peter's fear and doubt. Father, we plead for Your mercy and ask You to humble us and make us more devoted students of Jesus. His resolve to accomplish Your work has brought blessings to us all. Lead us to be more like our Savior.

THOUGHT QUESTIONS

Why did Peter lash out at the soldier? Can outbursts and quick reactions be a symptom of a faith that needs some work?

What are situations in your life where you need to have calm, confident responses like Jesus did throughout this chapter?

Pilate asks a fateful question: "What is truth?" Is Jesus the answer to that question for you, and what does He mean in your life?

JOHN 19

Pilate has Jesus scourged with whips and places a crown of thorns upon His head. He then parades Jesus before the Jews while openly claiming to find no guilt in Him. Even though Pilate makes efforts to release Jesus, the Jews threaten to report Pilate to Caesar unless he crucifies Him. Pilate relents and delivers Jesus over to death. He writes "The King of the Jews" over the Savior's cross, though the Jewish masses oppose this designation. Jesus is then crucified with His mother and other disciples looking on. He asks John to care for His mother after His passing. Jesus announces, "It is finished" and bows His head in death. Joseph and Nicodemus, two secret followers of Jesus, take Jesus's body and bury Him in a new tomb.

FOR MY BENEFIT

The central event of human history is the death of Jesus on the cross for our sins. Jesus had the power to prevent this. He tells Pilate he has no authority over Him. And yet, our Savior is willingly led like a lamb to the slaughter. John's gospel reveals three statements of Jesus on the cross, each revealing something about Him. His call to John to care for Mary shows Jesus' love for His own. He then said, "I am thirsty," indicating He physically suffered for us. When Jesus said, "It is finished," this proved that He was devoted to the Lord's will, even unto death. Jesus demonstrated love, sacrifice, and faith. These qualities live on in those who follow Him.

MY PRAYER

Holy Father, we praise You for sending Your Son to die in our place and to take away our sins. We see in Him deep love for others, a sacrificial spirit, and undying trust in You and Your plan to save souls. God, we are so grateful. But plant within us something more than just gratitude. Form within us the desire to live like Jesus in this world. Please help us develop selfless love for others, a willingness to pay the cost of discipleship, and a trust in You and Your will that cannot be diminished by anything or anyone.

THOUGHT QUESTIONS

Pilate is a tragic character. He knew Jesus was innocent but was too weak to stand up for Him. How are you stronger than Pilate?

_____

_____

Jesus had the power to stop His crucifixion. Why did He go through with it, and how can that same spirit be seen in your life?

_____

_____

Joseph and Nicodemus were disciples who emerged from secrecy. Are there areas in your life where it is time to do this as well?

_____

_____

JOHN 20

Early on Sunday morning, Mary Magdalene comes to the tomb and sees the stone rolled away. She goes to tell the apostles. Peter and John run to the tomb and see that it is empty. Not understanding Christ's resurrection, they return home. Mary then sees two angels sitting in the tomb. She turns around and sees Jesus alive and well! She returns to tell the disciples that she has spoken with Jesus. That evening, Jesus appears to ten of His apostles and gifts them with the Holy Spirit. Thomas was not with them and continues to have doubts. Eight days later, Jesus appears and shows Thomas the piercings in His hands and side. He then says great blessings will come to those who have not seen and yet believe.

FOR MY BENEFIT

The resurrection and appearance of Jesus is the most transformational moment in all of human history. From this victory comes undeniable proof of power over Satan, sin, and death. For us, living after Jesus was raised and ascended, we can see how much hope exists in Christ. However, on the day He was raised, the disciples still had many doubts that left them gripped in fear. Even after Mary reported seeing Jesus, the disciples did not fully believe. Thomas wrestled with doubt a week after Jesus was raised. They had much to learn. This is why John's gospel presents so much testimony for us: so that we will know the truth about Jesus and never live in fear and doubt.

MY PRAYER

Great Father, we believe. We believe the tomb was empty on the first day of the week. We believe Jesus overcame death and now lives as our risen and ruling Savior. Thank You for fulfilling Your promise to bring us hope through Your Son's victory over Satan. Like Mary clinging to Jesus after He appeared to her, we long to cling to our King and thank Him face-to-face for His sacrifice and love. Dear Lord, help us not to be burdened by doubt. May we always stay nourished in Scripture, believing the testimony about Christ, and enjoying life in His name.

THOUGHT QUESTIONS

Disciples throughout this chapter struggled to believe until they saw Jesus. How must your faith be even greater than theirs?

Jesus gifted the Holy Spirit to the apostles as well as the power to forgive sins. How obedient should you be to their teachings?

What does it mean to "believe that Jesus is the Christ, the Son of God, and that believing you may have life in His name"?

JOHN 21

Jesus appears a third time to His disciples, this time at the Sea of Tiberias. Peter, and several others, fish throughout the night and catch nothing. From the beach, Jesus tells them to lower their nets once again, and they come up with 153 fish. Peter jumps in and swims to see Jesus. The rest of the men also hurry back to the shore, and they all enjoy breakfast with Him. Jesus emphatically instructs Peter to show love for Him by tending His sheep, which is a reference to Christ's followers. Peter, along with all the apostles, would suffer, even to death, as they devote the rest of their lives to following Jesus. The author of this letter is John, who is one of the apostles with Jesus on that beach.

FOR MY BENEFIT

Jesus is the Son of God. He had just risen from the dead, and He was about to ascend into heaven. And yet, he took the time to visit disciples on the beach and have breakfast with them. He shared with them what He expected of them and what troubles would soon come. Our Savior is infinitely greater and more important than His followers, and yet He devotes time to them. He sits and eats with them. He shows great patience with them. This is our Lord, and this is how much He loves each one of us. What He asks in return is simple: love Him, help His people, and follow Him in whatever direction He leads us.

MY PRAYER

Great God of heaven, we have read the words of the Apostle John, an eyewitness to the life of Jesus, and we believe His testimony. From this letter, You have shown us that Jesus is Your Son, that He is both powerful and kind, and that He is worthy to be followed. He cares for us, and He has an important mission for our lives. Help us to know our mission, and to engage in it with the people You put in our path. Make us fishers of men and teach us how to help tend Your Son's sheep.

THOUGHT QUESTIONS

Jesus told Peter three times to "tend My sheep." How has the good Shepherd challenged us to take care of His sheep until He returns?

_____

_____

How should your relationship with Jesus resemble sitting with Him at breakfast, being taught how to serve Him and love others?

_____

_____

John could have written many more things about Jesus. But why did He write this Gospel, and what does it teach you about Christ?

_____

_____